The Seven Seas by Rudyard Kipling

Rudyard Kipling: A great Victorian, a great writer of Empire, a great man.

Rudyard Kipling was one of the most popular writers of prose and poetry in the late 19th and 20th Century and awarded the Noble Prize for Literature in 1907.

Born in Bombay on 30th December 1865, as was the custom in those days, he and his sister were sent back to England when he was 5. The ill-treatment and cruelty by the couple who they boarded with in Portsmouth, Kipling himself suggested, contributed to the onset of his literary life. This was further enhanced by his return to India at age 16 to work on a local paper, as not only did this result in him writing constantly but also made him explore issues of identity and national allegiance which pervade much of his work.

Whilst he is best remembered for his classic children's stories and his popular poem 'If...' he is also regarded as a major innovator in the art of the short story.

Index of Contents

To The City Of Bombay

The Cities are full of pride,
Challenging each to each—
This from her mountain-side,
That from her burthened beach.

They count their ships full tale—
Their corn and oil and wine,
Derrick and loom and bale,
And rampart's gun-flecked line;
City by city they hail:
"Hast aught to match with mine?"

And the men that breed from them
They traffic up and down,
But cling to their cities' hem
As a child to the mother's gown.

When they talk with the stranger bands,
Dazed and newly alone;
When they walk in the stranger lands,
By roaring streets unknown;
Blessing her where she stands
For strength above their own.

(On high to hold her fame
That stands all fame beyond,
By oath to back the same,
Most faithful-foolish-fond;
Making her mere-breathed name
Their bond upon their bond.)

So thank I God my birth
Fell not in isles aside—
Waste headlands of the earth,
Or warring tribes untried—
But that she lent me worth
And gave me right to pride.

Surely in toil or fray
Under an alien sky,
Comfort it is to say:

"Of no mean city am I."

(Neither by service nor fee
Come I to mine estate—
Mother of Cities to me,
For I was born in her gate,
Between the palms and the sea,
Where the world-end steamers wait.)

Now for this debt I owe,
And for her far-borne cheer
Must I make haste and go
With tribute to her pier.

And she shall touch and remit
After the use of kings
(Orderly, ancient, fit)
My deep-sea plunderings,
And purchase in all lands.
And this we do for a sign
Her power is over mine,
And mine I hold at her hands.

A SONG OF THE ENGLISH

Fair is our lot—O goodly is our heritage!
(Humble ye, my people, and be fearful in your mirth!)
For the Lord our God Most High
He hath made the deep as dry,
He hath smote for us a pathway to the ends of all the Earth!

Yea, though we sinned—and our rulers went from righteousness—
Deep in all dishonour though we stained our garments' hem.
Oh be ye not dismayed,
Though we stumbled and we strayed,
We were led by evil counsellors—the Lord shall deal with them.

Hold ye the Faith—the Faith our Fathers sealèd us;
Whoring not with visions—overwise and overstale.
Except ye pay the Lord
Single heart and single sword,
Of your children in their bondage shall He ask them treble-tale.

Keep ye the Law—be swift in all obedience.
Clear the land of evil, drive the road and bridge the ford.
Make ye sure to each his own

That he reap what he hath sown;
By the peace among Our peoples let men know we serve the Lord.

Hear now a song—a song of broken interludes—
A song of little cunning; of a singer nothing worth.
Through the naked words and mean
May ye see the truth between
As the singer knew and touched it in the ends of all the Earth!

The Coastwise Lights

Our brows are wreathed with spindrift and the weed is on our knees;
Our loins are battered 'neath us by the swinging, smoking seas.
From reef and rock and skerry—over headland, ness and voe—
The Coastwise Lights of England watch the ships of England go!

Through the endless summer evenings, on the lineless, level floors;
Through the yelling Channel tempest when the syren hoots and roars—
By day the dipping house-flag and by night the rocket's trail—
As the sheep that graze behind us so we know them where they hail.

We bridge across the dark, and bid the helmsman have a care,
The flash that wheeling inland wakes his sleeping wife to prayer;
From our vexed eyries, head to gale, we bind in burning chains
The lover from the sea-rim drawn—his love in English lanes.

We greet the clippers wing-and-wing that race the Southern wool;
We warn the crawling cargo-tanks of Bremen, Leith and Hull;
To each and all our equal lamp at peril of the sea—
The white wall-sided warships or the whalers of Dundee!

Come up, come in from Eastward, from the guard-ports of the Morn!
Beat up, beat in from Southerly, O gipsies of the Horn!
Swift shuttles of an Empire's loom that weave us main to main,
The Coastwise Lights of England give you welcome back again!

Go, get you gone up-Channel with the sea-crust on your plates;
Go, get you into London with the burden of your freights!
Haste, for they talk of Empire there, and say, if any seek,
The Lights of England sent you and by silence shall ye speak.

The Song of the Dead

Hear now the Song of the Dead—in the North by the torn berg-edges—
They that look still to the Pole, asleep by their hide-stripped sledges.
Song of the Dead in the South—in the sun by their skeleton horses,

Where the warrigal whimpers and bays through the dust of the sere river-courses.

Song of the Dead in the East—in the heat-rotted jungle hollows,
Where the dog-ape barks in the kloof—in the brake of the buffalo-wallows.
Song of the Dead in the West—in the Barrens, the snow that betrayed them,
Where the wolverine tumbles their packs from the camp and the grave-mound they made them;

Hear now the Song of the Dead!

I

We were dreamers, dreaming greatly, in the man-stifled town;
We yearned beyond the skyline where the strange roads go down.
Came the Whisper, came the Vision, came the Power with the Need.
Till the Soul that is not man's soul was lent us to lead.
As the deer breaks—as the steer breaks—from the herd where they graze,
In the faith of little children we went on our ways.
Then the wood failed—then the food failed—then the last water dried—
In the faith of little children we lay down and died.
On the sand-drift—on the veldt-side—in the fern-scrub we lay,
That our sons might follow after by the bones on the way.
Follow after—follow after! We have watered the root,
And the bud has come to blossom that ripens for fruit!
Follow after—we are waiting by the trails that we lost
For the sound of many footsteps, for the tread of a host.
Follow after—follow after—for the harvest is sown:
By the bones about the wayside ye shall come to your own!

When Drake went down to the Horn
And England was crowned thereby,
'Twixt seas unsailed and shores unhailed
Our Lodge—our Lodge was born
(And England was crowned thereby).

Which never shall close again
By day nor yet by night,
While man shall take his life to stake
At risk of shoal or main
(By day nor yet by night),

But standeth even so
As now we witness here,
While men depart, of joyful heart,
Adventure for to know.
(As now bear witness here).

We have fed our sea for a thousand years
And she calls us, still unfed,
Though there's never a wave of all her waves
But marks our English dead:
We have strawed our best to the weed's unrest
To the shark and the sheering gull.
If blood be the price of admiralty,
Lord God, we ha' paid in full!

There's never a flood goes shoreward now
But lifts a keel we manned;
There's never an ebb goes seaward now
But drops our dead on the sand—
But slinks our dead on the sands forlore,
From The Ducies to the Swin.
If blood be the price of admiralty,
If blood be the price of admiralty,
Lord God, we ha' paid it in!

We must feed our sea for a thousand years,
For that is our doom and pride,
As it was when they sailed with the Golden Hind
Or the wreck that struck last tide—
Or the wreck that lies on the spouting reef
Where the ghastly blue-lights flare.
If blood be the price of admiralty,
If blood be the price of admiralty,
If blood be the price of admiralty,
Lord God, we ha' bought it fair!

The Deep-sea Cables

The wrecks dissolve above us; their dust drops down from afar—
Down to the dark, to the utter dark, where the blind white sea-snakes are.
There is no sound, no echo of sound, in the deserts of the deep,
Or the great gray level plains of ooze where the shell-burred cables creep.

Here in the womb of the world—here on the tie-ribs of earth
Words, and the words of men, flicker and flutter and beat—
Warning, sorrow and gain, salutation and mirth—
For a Power troubles the Still that has neither voice nor feet.

They have wakened the timeless Things; they have killed their father Time;
Joining hands in the gloom, a league from the last of the sun.
Hush! Men talk to-day o'er the waste of the ultimate slime,

And a new Word runs between: whispering, "Let us be one!"

The Song of the Sons

One from the ends of the earth—gifts at an open door—
Treason has much, but we, Mother, thy sons have more!
From the whine of a dying man, from the snarl of a wolf-pack freed,
Turn, for the world is thine. Mother, be proud of thy seed!
Count, are we feeble or few? Hear, is our speech so rude?
Look, are we poor in the land? Judge, are we men of The Blood?

Those that have stayed at thy knees, Mother, go call them in—
We that were bred overseas wait and would speak with our kin.
Not in the dark do we fight—haggle and flout and gibe;
Selling our love for a price, loaning our hearts for a bribe.
Gifts have we only to-day—Love without promise or fee—
Hear, for thy children speak, from the uttermost parts of the sea:

The Song of the Cities

Bombay

Royal and Dower-royal, I the Queen
Fronting thy richest sea with richer hands—
A thousand mills roar through me where I glean
All races from all lands.

Calcutta

Me the Sea-captain loved, the River built,
Wealth sought and Kings adventured life to hold.
Hail, England! I am Asia—Power on silt,
Death in my hands, but Gold!

Madras

Clive kissed me on the mouth and eyes and brow,
Wonderful kisses, so that I became
Crowned above Queens—a withered beldame now,
Brooding on ancient fame.

Rangoon

Hail, Mother! Do they call me rich in trade?
Little care I, but hear the shorn priest drone,
And watch my silk-clad lovers, man by maid,
Laugh 'neath my Shwe Dagon.

Singapore

Hail, Mother! East and West must seek my aid
Ere the spent gear shall dare the ports afar.
The second doorway of the wide world's trade
Is mine to loose or bar.

Hong-Kong

Hail, Mother! Hold me fast; my Praya sleeps
Under innumerable keels to-day.
Yet guard (and landward) or to-morrow sweeps
Thy warships down the bay.

Halifax

Into the mist my guardian prows put forth,
Behind the mist my virgin ramparts lie,
The Warden of the Honour of the North,
Sleepless and veiled am I!

Quebec and Montreal

Peace is our portion. Yet a whisper rose,
Foolish and causeless, half in jest, half hate.
Now wake we and remember mighty blows,
And, fearing no man, wait!

Victoria

From East to West the circling word has passed,
Till West is East beside our land-locked blue;
From East to West the tested chain holds fast,
The well-forged link rings true!

Capetown

Hail! Snatched and bartered oft from hand to hand,
I dream my dream, by rock and heath and pine,
Of Empire to the northward. Ay, one land
From Lion's Head to Line!

Melbourne.
Greeting! Nor fear nor favour won us place,
Got between greed of gold and dread of drouth,
Loud-voiced and reckless as the wild tide-race
That whips our harbour-mouth!

Sydney

Greeting! My birth-stain have I turned to good;
Forcing strong wills perverse to steadfastness;
The first flush of the tropics in my blood,
And at my feet Success!

Brisbane

The northern stirp beneath the southern skies—
I build a nation for an Empire's need,
Suffer a little, and my land shall rise,
Queen over lands indeed!

Hobart

Man's love first found me; man's hate made me Hell;
For my babes' sake I cleansed those infamies.
Earnest for leave to live and labour well
God flung me peace and ease.

Auckland

Last, loneliest, loveliest, exquisite, apart—
On us, on us the unswerving season smiles,
Who wonder 'mid our fern why men depart
To seek the Happy Isles!

England's Answer

Truly ye come of The Blood; slower to bless than to ban;

Little used to lie down at the bidding of any man.
Flesh of the flesh that I bred, bone of the bone that I bare;
Stark as your sons shall be—stern as your fathers were.
Deeper than speech our love, stronger than life our tether,
But we do not fall on the neck nor kiss when we come together.
My arm is nothing weak, my strength is not gone by;
Sons, I have borne many sons but my dugs are not dry.
Look, I have made ye a place and opened wide the doors,
That ye may talk together, your Barons and Councillors—
Wards of the Outer March, Lords of the Lower Seas,
Ay, talk to your gray mother that bore you on her knees!—
That ye may talk together, brother to brother's face—
Thus for the good of your peoples—thus for the Pride of the Race.
Also, we will make promise. So long as The Blood endures,
I shall know that your good is mine: ye shall feel that my strength is yours:
In the day of Armageddon, at the last great fight of all,
That Our House stand together and the pillars do not fall.
Draw now the three-fold knot firm on the nine-fold bands,
And the Law that ye make shall be law after the rule of your lands.
This for the waxen Heath, and that for the Wattle-bloom,
This for the Maple-leaf, and that for the southern Broom.
The Law that ye make shall be law and I do not press my will,
Because ye are Sons of The Blood and call me Mother still.
Now must ye speak to your kinsmen and they must speak to you,
After the use of the English, in straight-flung words and few.
Go to your work and be strong, halting not in your ways,
Baulking the end half-won for an instant dole of praise.
Stand to your work and be wise—certain of sword and pen,
Who are neither children nor Gods, but men in a world of men!

THE FIRST CHANTEY

Mine was the woman to me, darkling I found her;
Haling her dumb from the camp, held her and bound her.
Hot rose her tribe on our track ere I had proved her;
Hearing her laugh in the gloom, greatly I loved her.

Swift through the forest we ran; none stood to guard us,
Few were my people and far; then the flood barred us—
Him we call Son of the Sea, sullen and swollen;
Panting we waited the death, stealer and stolen,

Yet ere they came to my lance laid for the slaughter,
Lightly she leaped to a log lapped in the water;
Holding on high and apart skins that arrayed her,
Called she the God of the Wind that he should aid her.

Life had the tree at that word, (Praise we the Giver!)
Otter-like left he the bank for the full river.
Far fell their axes behind, flashing and ringing,
Wonder was on me and fear, yet she was singing.

Low lay the land we had left. Now the blue bound us,
Even the Floor of the Gods level around us.
Whisper there was not, nor word, shadow nor showing,
Still the light stirred on the deep, glowing and growing.

Then did He leap to His place flaring from under,
He the Compeller, the Sun, bared to our wonder.
Nay, not a league from our eyes blinded with gazing,
Cleared He the womb of the world, huge and amazing!

This we beheld (and we live)—the Pit of the Burning,
Then the God spoke to the tree for our returning;
Back to the beach of our flight, fearless and slowly,
Back to our slayers he went: but we were holy.

Men that were hot in that hunt, women that followed,
Babes that were promised our bones, trembled and wallowed:
Over the necks of the tribe crouching and fawning—
Prophet and priestess we came back from the dawning!

THE LAST CHANTEY

"And there was no more sea."

Thus said The Lord in the Vault above the Cherubim,
Calling to the angels and the souls in their degree:
"Lo! Earth has passed away
On the smoke of Judgment Day.
That Our word may be established shall We gather up the sea?"

Loud sang the souls of the jolly, jolly mariners:
"Plague upon the hurricane that made us furl and flee!
But the war is done between us,
In the deep the Lord hath seen us—
Our bones we'll leave the barracout', and God may sink the sea!"

Then said the soul of Judas that betrayèd Him:
"Lord, hast Thou forgotten Thy covenant with me?
How once a year I go
To cool me on the floe,

And Ye take my day of mercy if Ye take away the sea!"

Then said the soul of the Angel of the Off-shore Wind:
(He that bits the thunder when the bull-mouthed breakers flee):
"I have watch and ward to keep
O'er Thy wonders on the deep,
And Ye take mine honour from me if Ye take away the sea!"

Loud sang the souls of the jolly, jolly mariners:
"Nay, but we were angry, and a hasty folk are we!
If we worked the ship together
Till she foundered in foul weather,
Are we babes that we should clamour for a vengeance on the sea?"

Then said the souls of the slaves that men threw overboard:
"Kennelled in the picaroon a weary band were we;
But Thy arm was strong to save,
And it touched us on the wave,
And we drowsed the long tides idle till Thy Trumpets tore the sea."

Then cried the soul of the stout Apostle Paul to God:
"Once we frapped a ship, and she laboured woundily.
There were fourteen score of these,
And they blessed Thee on their knees,
When they learned Thy Grace and Glory under Malta by the sea."

Loud sang the souls of the jolly, jolly mariners,
Plucking at their harps, and they plucked unhandily:
"Our thumbs are rough and tarred,
And the tune is something hard—
May we lift a Deep-sea Chantey such as seamen use at sea?"

Then said the souls of the gentlemen-adventurers—
Fettered wrist to bar all for red iniquity:
"Ho, we revel in our chains
O'er the sorrow that was Spain's;
Heave or sink it, leave or drink it, we were masters of the sea!"

Up spake the soul of a gray Gothavn 'speckshioner—
(He that led the flinching in the fleets of fair Dundee):
"Ho, the ringer and right whale,
And the fish we struck for sale,
Will Ye whelm them all for wantonness that wallow in the sea?"

Loud sang the souls of the jolly, jolly mariners,
Crying: "Under Heaven, here is neither lead nor lea!
Must we sing for evermore
On the windless, glassy floor?

Take back your golden fiddles and we'll beat to open sea!"

Then stooped the Lord, and He called the good sea up to Him,
And 'stablished his borders unto all eternity,
That such as have no pleasure
For to praise the Lord by measure,
They may enter into galleons and serve Him on the sea.

Sun, wind, and cloud shall fail not from the face of it,
Stinging, ringing spindrift, nor the fulmar flying free;
And the ships shall go abroad
To the glory of the Lord
Who heard the silly sailor-folk and gave them back their sea!

THE MERCHANTMEN

King Solomon drew merchantmen,
Because of his desire
For peacocks, apes, and ivory,
From Tarshish unto Tyre:
With cedars out of Lebanon
Which Hiram rafted down,
But we be only sailormen
That use in London town.

Coastwise—cross-seas—round the world and back again—
Where the flaw shall head us or the full Trade suits—
Plain-sail—storm-sail—lay your board and tack again—
And that's the way we'll pay Paddy Doyle for his boots!

We bring no store of ingots,
Of spice or precious stones,
But that we have we gathered
With sweat and aching bones:
In flame beneath the tropics,
In frost upon the floe,
And jeopardy of every wind
That does between them go.

And some we got by purchase,
And some we had by trade,
And some we found by courtesy
Of pike and carronade,
At midnight, 'mid-sea meetings,
For charity to keep,
And light the rolling homeward-bound

That rode a foot too deep.

By sport of bitter weather
We're walty, strained, and scarred
From the kentledge on the kelson
To the slings upon the yard.
Six oceans had their will of us
To carry all away—
Our galley 's in the Baltic,
And our boom 's in Mossel Bay!

We've floundered off the Texel,
Awash with sodden deals,
We've slipped from Valparaiso
With the Norther at our heels:
We've ratched beyond the Crossets
That tusk the Southern Pole,
And dipped our gunnels under
To the dread Agulhas roll.

Beyond all outer charting
We sailed where none have sailed,
And saw the land-lights burning
On islands none have hailed;
Our hair stood up for wonder,
But, when the night was done,
There danced the deep to windward
Blue-empty 'neath the sun!

Strange consorts rode beside us
And brought us evil luck;
The witch-fire climbed our channels,
And danced on vane and truck:
Till, through the red tornado,
That lashed us nigh to blind,
We saw The Dutchman plunging,
Full canvas, head to wind!

We've heard the Midnight Leadsman
That calls the black deep down—
Ay, thrice we've heard The Swimmer,
The Thing that may not drown.
On frozen bunt and gasket
The sleet-cloud drave her hosts,
When, manned by more than signed with us,
We passed the Isle o' Ghosts!

And north, amid the hummocks,

A biscuit-toss below,
We met the silent shallop
That frighted whalers know;
For, down a cruel ice-lane,
That opened as he sped,
We saw dead Henry Hudson
Steer, North by West, his dead.

So dealt God's waters with us
Beneath the roaring skies,
So walked His signs and marvels
All naked to our eyes:
But we were heading homeward
With trade to lose or make—
Good Lord, they slipped behind us
In the tailing of our wake!

Let go, let go the anchors;
Now shamed at heart are we
To bring so poor a cargo home
That had for gift the sea!
Let go the great bow-anchors—
Ah, fools were we and blind—
The worst we baled with utter toil,
The best we left behind!

Coastwise—cross-seas—round the world and back again,
Whither the flaw shall fail us or the Trades drive down:
Plain-sail—storm-sail—lay your board and tack again—
And all to bring a cargo up to London Town!

McANDREWS' HYMN

Lord, Thou hast made this world below the shadow of a dream,
An', taught by time, I tak' it so—exceptin' always Steam.
From coupler-flange to spindle-guide I see Thy Hand, O God—
Predestination in the stride o' yon connectin'-rod.
John Calvin might ha' forged the same—enorrmous, certain, slow—
Ay, wrought it in the furnace-flame—my "Institutio."
I cannot get my sleep to-night; old bones are hard to please;
I'll stand the middle watch up here—alone wi' God an' these
My engines, after ninety days o' race an' rack an' strain
Through all the seas of all Thy world, slam-bangin' home again.
Slam-bang too much—they knock a wee—the crosshead-gibs are loose;
But thirty thousand mile o' sea has gied them fair excuse....
Fine, clear an' dark—a full-draught breeze, wi' Ushant out o' sight,

An' Ferguson relievin' Hay. Old girl, ye'll walk to-night!
His wife's at Plymouth.... Seventy—One—Two—Three since he began—
Three turns for Mistress Ferguson ... an' who's to blame the man?
There's none at any port for me, by drivin' fast or slow,
Since Elsie Campbell went to Thee, Lord, thirty years ago.
(The year the Sarah Sands was burned. Oh roads we used to tread,
Fra' Maryhill to Pollokshaws—fra' Govan to Parkhead!)
Not but they're ceevil on the Board. Ye'll hear Sir Kenneth say:
"Good morrn, McAndrews! Back again? An' how's your bilge to-day?"
Miscallin' technicalities but handin' me my chair
To drink Madeira wi' three Earls—the auld Fleet Engineer,
That started as a boiler-whelp—when steam and he were low.
I mind the time we used to serve a broken pipe wi' tow.
Ten pound was all the pressure then—Eh! Eh!—a man wad drive;
An' here, our workin' gauges give one hunder' fifty-five!
We're creepin' on wi' each new rig—less weight an' larger power:
There'll be the loco-boiler next an' thirty knots an hour!
Thirty an' more. What I ha' seen since ocean-steam began
Leaves me no doot for the machine: but what about the man?
The man that counts, wi' all his runs, one million mile o' sea:
Four time the span from earth to moon.... How far, O Lord, from Thee?
That wast beside him night an' day. Ye mind my first typhoon?
It scoughed the skipper on his way to jock wi' the saloon.
Three feet were on the stokehold floor—just slappin' to an' fro—
An' cast me on a furnace-door. I have the marks to show.
Marks! I ha' marks o' more than burns—deep in my soul an' black,
An' times like this, when things go smooth, my wickudness comes back.
The sins o' four and forty years, all up an' down the seas,
Clack an' repeat like valves half-fed.... Forgie's our trespasses.
Nights when I'd come on deck to mark, wi' envy in my gaze,
The couples kittlin' in the dark between the funnel stays;
Years when I raked the ports wi' pride to fill my cup o' wrong—
Judge not, O Lord, my steps aside at Gay Street in Hong-Kong!
Blot out the wastrel hours of mine in sin when I abode—
Jane Harrigan's an' Number Nine, The Reddick an' Grant Road!
An' waur than all—my crownin' sin—rank blasphemy an' wild.
I was not four and twenty then—Ye wadna' judge a child?
I'd seen the Tropics first that run—new fruit, new smells, new air—
How could I tell—blind-fou wi' sun—the Deil was lurkin' there?
By day like playhouse-scenes the shore slid past our sleepy eyes;
By night those soft, lasceevious stars leered from those velvet skies,
In port (we used no cargo-steam) I'd daunder down the streets—
An ijjit grinnin' in a dream—for shells an' parrakeets,
An' walkin'-sticks o' carved bamboo an' blowfish stuffed an' dried—
Fillin' my bunk wi' rubbishry the Chief put overside.
Till, off Sumbawa Head, Ye mind, I heard a land-breeze ca'
Milk-warm wi' breath o' spice an' bloom: "McAndrews, come awa'!"
Firm, clear an' low—no haste, no hate—the ghostly whisper went,

Just statin' eevidential facts beyon' all argument:
"Your mither's God's a graspin' deil, the shadow o' yoursel',
Got out o' books by meenisters clean daft on Heaven an' Hell.
They mak' him in the Broomielaw, o' Glasgie cold an' dirt,
A jealous, pridefu' fetich, lad, that's only strong to hurt,
Ye'll not go back to Him again an' kiss His red-hot rod,
But come wi' Us" (Now, who were They?) "an' know the Leevin' God,
That does not kipper souls for sport or break a life in jest,
But swells the ripenin' cocoanuts an' ripes the woman's breast."
An' there it stopped: cut off: no more; that quiet, certain voice—
For me, six months o' twenty-four, to leave or take at choice.
'Twas on me like a thunderclap—it racked me through an' through—
Temptation past the show o' speech, unnamable an' new—
The Sin against the Holy Ghost?... An' under all, our screw.
That storm blew by but left behind her anchor-shiftin' swell,
Thou knowest all my heart an' mind, Thou knowest, Lord, I fell.
Third on the Mary Gloster then, and first that night in Hell!
Yet was Thy hand beneath my head: about my feet Thy care—
Fra' Deli clear to Torres Strait, the trial o' despair,
But when we touched the Barrier Reef Thy answer to my prayer!
We dared na run that sea by night but lay an' held our fire,
An' I was drowzin' on the hatch—sick—sick wi' doubt an' tire:
"Better the sight of eyes that see than wanderin' o' desire!"
Ye mind that word? Clear as our gongs—again, an' once again,
When rippin' down through coral-trash ran out our moorin'-chain;
An' by Thy Grace I had the Light to see my duty plain.
Light on the engine-room—no more—clear as our carbons burn.
I've lost it since a thousand times, but never past return.

Obsairve! Per annum we'll have here two thousand souls aboard—
Think not I dare to justify myself before the Lord,
But—average fifteen hunder' souls safe-borne fra' port to port—
I am o' service to my kind. Ye wadna' blame the thought?
Maybe they steam from grace to wrath—to sin by folly led,—
It isna mine to judge their path—their lives are on my head.
Mine at the last—when all is done it all comes back to me,
The fault that leaves six thousand ton a log upon the sea.
We'll tak' one stretch—three weeks an' odd by any road ye steer—
Fra' Cape Town east to Wellington—ye need an engineer.
Fail there—ye've time to weld your shaft—ay, eat it, ere ye're spoke,
Or make Kerguelen under sail—three jiggers burned wi' smoke!
An' home again, the Rio run: it's no child's play to go
Steamin' to bell for fourteen days o' snow an' floe an' blow—
The bergs like kelpies overside that girn an' turn an' shift
Whaur, grindin' like the Mills o' God, goes by the big South drift.
(Hail, snow an' ice that praise the Lord: I've met them at their work,
An' wished we had anither route or they anither kirk.)
Yon's strain, hard strain, o' head an' hand, for though Thy Power brings

All skill to naught, Ye'll understand a man must think o' things.
Then, at the last, we'll get to port an' hoist their baggage clear—
The passengers, wi' gloves an' canes—an' this is what I'll hear:
"Well, thank ye for a pleasant voyage. The tender's comin' now."
While I go testin' follower-bolts an' watch the skipper bow.
They've words for everyone but me—shake hands wi' half the crew,
Except the dour Scots engineer, the man they never knew.
An' yet I like the wark for all we've dam' few pickin's here—
No pension, an' the most we earn's four hunder' pound a year.
Better myself abroad? Maybe. I'd sooner starve than sail
Wi' such as call a snifter-rod ross.... French for nightingale.
Commeesion on my stores? Some do; but I can not afford
To lie like stewards wi' patty-pans. I'm older than the Board.
A bonus on the coal I save? Ou ay, the Scots are close,
But when I grudge the strength Ye gave I'll grudge their food to those.
(There's bricks that I might recommend—an' clink the fire-bars cruel.
No! Welsh—Wangarti at the worst—an' damn all patent fuel!)
Inventions? Ye must stay in port to mak' a patent pay.
My Deeferential Valve-Gear taught me how that business lay,
I blame no chaps wi' clearer head for aught they make or sell.
I found that I could not invent an' look to these—as well.
So, wrestled wi' Apollyon—Nah!—fretted like a bairn—
But burned the workin'-plans last run wi' all I hoped to earn.
Ye know how hard an Idol dies, an' what that meant to me—
E'en tak' it for a sacrifice acceptable to Thee....
Below there! Oiler! What's your wark? Ye find her runnin' hard?
Ye needn't swill the cap wi' oil—this isn't the Cunard.
Ye thought? Ye are not paid to think. Go, sweat that off again!
Tck! Tck! It's deeficult to sweer nor tak' The Name in vain!
Men, ay an' women, call me stern. Wi' these to oversee
Ye'll note I've little time to burn on social repartee.
The bairns see what their elders miss; they'll hunt me to an' fro,
Till for the sake of—well, a kiss—I tak' 'em down below.
That minds me of our Viscount loon—Sir Kenneth's kin—the chap
Wi' russia leather tennis-shoon an' spar-decked yachtin'-cap.
I showed him round last week, o'er all—an' at the last says he:
"Mister McAndrews, don't you think steam spoils romance at sea?"
Damned ijjit! I'd been doon that morn to see what ailed the throws,
Manholin', on my back—the cranks three inches from my nose.
Romance! Those first-class passengers they like it very well,
Printed an' bound in little books; but why don't poets tell?
I'm sick of all their quirks an' turns—the loves an' doves they dream—
Lord, send a man like Robbie Burns to sing the Song o' Steam!
To match wi' Scotia's noblest speech yon orchestra sublime
Whaurto—uplifted like the Just—the tail-rods mark the time.
The crank-throws give the double-bass; the feed-pump sobs an' heaves:
An' now the main eccentrics start their quarrel on the sheaves.
Her time, her own appointed time, the rocking link-head bides,

Till—hear that note?—the rod's return whings glimmerin' through the guides.
They're all awa'! True beat, full power, the clangin' chorus goes
Clear to the tunnel where they sit, my purrin' dynamoes.
Interdependence absolute, foreseen, ordained, decreed,
To work, Ye'll note, at any tilt an' every rate o' speed.
Fra' skylight-lift to furnace-bars, backed, bolted, braced an' stayed,
An' singin' like the Mornin' Stars for joy that they are made;
While, out o' touch o' vanity, the sweatin' thrust-block says:
"Not unto us the praise, or man—not unto us the praise!"
Now, a' together, hear them lift their lesson—theirs an' mine:
"Law, Orrder, Duty an' Restraint, Obedience, Discipline!"
Mill, forge an' try-pit taught them that when roarin' they arose,
An' whiles I wonder if a soul was gied them wi' the blows.
Oh for a man to weld it then, in one trip-hammer strain,
Till even first-class passengers could tell the meanin' plain!
But no one cares except mysel' that serve an' understand
My seven thousand horse-power here. Eh, Lord! They're grand—they're grand!
Uplift am I? When first in store the new-made beasties stood,
Were Ye cast down that breathed the Word declarin' all things good?
Not so! O' that warld-liftin' joy no after-fall could vex,
Ye've left a glimmer still to cheer the Man—the Arrtifex!
That holds, in spite o' knock and scale, o' friction, waste an' slip,
An' by that light—now, mark my word—we'll build the Perfect Ship.
I'll never last to judge her lines or take her curve—not I.
But I ha' lived an' I ha' worked. All thanks to Thee, Most High!
An' I ha' done what I ha' done—judge Thou if ill or well—
Always Thy Grace preventin' me....
Losh! Yon's the "Stand by" bell.
Pilot so soon? His flare it is. The mornin'-watch is set.
Well, God be thanked, as I was sayin', I'm no Pelagian yet.
Now I'll tak' on....
'Morrn, Ferguson. Man, have ye ever thought
What your good leddy costs in coal?... I'll burn 'em down to port.

THE MIRACLES

I sent a message to my dear—
A thousand leagues and more to her—
The dumb sea-levels thrilled to hear,
And Lost Atlantis bore to her.

Behind my message hard I came,
And nigh had found a grave for me;
But that I launched of steel and flame
Did war against the wave for me.

Uprose the deep, by gale on gale,
To bid me change my mind again—
He broke his teeth along my rail,
And, roaring, swung behind again.

I stayed the sun at noon to tell
My way across the waste of it;
I read the storm before it fell
And made the better haste of it.

Afar, I hailed the land at night—
The towers I built had heard of me—
And, ere my rocket reached its height,
Had flashed my Love the word of me.

Earth gave her chosen men of strength
(They lived and strove and died for me)
To drive my road a nation's length,
And toss the miles aside for me.

I snatched their toil to serve my needs—
Too slow their fleetest flew for me—
I tired twenty smoking steeds,
And bade them bait a new for me.

I sent the lightnings forth to see
Where hour by hour she waited me.
Among ten million one was she,
And surely all men hated me!

Dawn ran to meet us at my goal—
Ah, day no tongue shall tell again!—
And little folk of little soul
Rose up to buy and sell again!

THE NATIVE-BORN

We've drunk to the Queen—God bless her!—
We've drunk to our mothers' land;
We've drunk to our English brother
(But he does not understand);
We've drunk to the wide creation,
And the Cross swings low to the morn,
Last toast, and of obligation,
A health to the Native-born!

They change their skies above them,
But not their hearts that roam!
We learned from our wistful mothers
To call old England "home";
We read of the English sky-lark,
Of the spring in the English lanes,
But we screamed with the painted lories
As we rode on the dusty plains!

They passed with their old-world legends—
Their tales of wrong and dearth—
Our fathers held by purchase,
But we by the right of birth;
Our heart's where they rocked our cradle,
Our love where we spent our toil,
And our faith and our hope and our honour
We pledge to our native soil!

I charge you charge your glasses—
I charge you drink with me
To the men of the Four New Nations,
And the Islands of the Sea—
To the last least lump of coral
That none may stand outside,
And our own good pride shall teach us
To praise our comrade's pride.

To the hush of the breathless morning
On the thin, tin, crackling roofs,
To the haze of the burned back-ranges
And the dust of the shoeless hoofs—
To the risk of a death by drowning,
To the risk of a death by drouth—
To the men of a million acres,
To the Sons of the Golden South.

To the Sons of the Golden South, (Stand up!)
And the life we live and know,
Let a fellow sing o' the little things he cares about,
If a fellow fights for the little things he cares about
With the weight of a single blow!

To the smoke of a hundred coasters,
To the sheep on a thousand hills,
To the sun that never blisters,
To the rain that never chills—
To the land of the waiting springtime,
To our five-meal, meat-fed men,

To the tall deep-bosomed women,
And the children nine and ten!

And the children nine and ten, (Stand up!)
And the life we live and know,
Let a fellow sing o' the little things he cares about,
If a fellow fights for the little things he cares about
With the weight of a two-fold blow!

To the far-flung fenceless prairie
Where the quick cloud-shadows trail,
To our neighbour's barn in the offing
And the line of the new-cut rail;
To the plough in her league-long furrow
With the gray Lake gulls behind—
To the weight of a half-year's winter
And the warm wet western wind!

To the home of the floods and thunder,
To her pale dry healing blue—
To the lift of the great Cape combers,
And the smell of the baked Karroo.
To the growl of the sluicing stamp-head—
To the reef and the water-gold,
To the last and the largest Empire,
To the map that is half unrolled!

To our dear dark foster-mothers,
To the heathen songs they sung—
To the heathen speech we babbled
Ere we came to the white man's tongue.
To the cool of our deep verandas—
To the blaze of our jewelled main,
To the night, to the palms in the moonlight,
And the fire-fly in the cane!

To the hearth of our people's people—
To her well-ploughed windy sea,
To the hush of our dread high-altars
Where the Abbey makes us We;
To the grist of the slow-ground ages,
To the gain that is yours and mine—
To the Bank of the Open Credit,
To the Power-house of the Line!

We've drunk to the Queen—God bless her!—
We've drunk to our mothers' land;
We've drunk to our English brother

(And we hope he'll understand).
We've drunk as much as we're able,
And the Cross swings low to the morn;
Last toast—and your foot on the table!—
A health to the Native-born!

A health to the Native-born, (Stand up!)
We're six white men arow,
All bound to sing o' the little things we care about,
All bound to fight for the little things we care about
With the weight of a six-fold blow!
By the might of our cable-tow, (Take hands!)
From the Orkneys to the Horn,
All round the world (and a little loop to pull it by),
All round the world (and a little strap to buckle it),
A health to the Native-born!

THE KING

"Farewell, Romance!" the Cave-men said;
"With bone well carved he went away,
Flint arms the ignoble arrowhead,
And jasper tips the spear to-day.
Changed are the Gods of Hunt and Dance,
And he with these. Farewell, Romance!"

"Farewell, Romance!" the Lake-folk sighed;
"We lift the weight of flatling years;
The caverns of the mountain side
Hold him who scorns our hutted piers.
Lost hills whereby we dare not dwell,
Guard ye his rest. Romance, farewell!"

"Farewell, Romance!" the Soldier spoke;
"By sleight of sword we may not win,
But scuffle 'mid uncleanly smoke
Of arquebus and culverin.
Honour is lost, and none may tell
Who paid good blows. Romance, farewell!"

"Farewell, Romance!" the Traders cried;
"Our keels ha' lain with every sea;
The dull-returning wind and tide
Heave up the wharf where we would be;
The known and noted breezes swell
Our trudging sail. Romance, farewell!"

"Good-bye, Romance!" the Skipper said;
"He vanished with the coal we burn;
Our dial marks full steam ahead,
Our speed is timed to half a turn.
Sure as the tidal trains we ply
'Twixt port and port. Romance, good-bye!"

"Romance!" the Season-tickets mourn,
"He never ran to catch his train,
But passed with coach and guard and horn—
And left the local—late again!
Confound Romance!"... And all unseen
Romance brought up the nine-fifteen.

His hand was on the lever laid,
His oil-can soothed the worrying cranks,
His whistle waked the snowbound grade,
His fog-horn cut the reeking Banks;
In dock and deep and mine and mill
The Boy-god reckless laboured still.

Robed, crowned and throned, he wove his spell,
Where heart-blood beat or hearth-smoke curled,
With unconsidered miracle,
Hedged in a backward-gazing world;
Then taught his chosen bard to say:
"The King was with us—yesterday!"

THE RHYME OF THE THREE SEALERS

Away by the lands of the Japanee,
When the paper lanterns glow
And the crews of all the shipping drink
In the house of Blood Street Joe,
At twilight, when the landward breeze
Brings up the harbour noise,
And ebb of Yokohama Bay
Swigs chattering through the buoys,
In Cisco's Dewdrop Dining Rooms
They tell the tale anew
Of a hidden sea and a hidden fight,
When the Baltic ran from the Northern Light
And the Stralsund fought the two!

Now this is the Law of the Muscovite, that he proves with shot and steel,

When ye come by his isles in the Smoky Sea ye must not take the seal,
Where the gray sea goes nakedly between the weed-hung shelves,
And the little blue fox he is bred for his skin and the seal they breed for themselves;
For when the matkas seek the shore to drop their pups aland,
The great man-seal haul out of the sea, aroaring, band by band;
And when the first September gales have slaked their rutting-wrath,
The great man-seal haul back to the sea and no man knows their path.
Then dark they lie and stark they lie—rookery, dune, and floe,
And the Northern Lights come down o' nights to dance with the houseless snow.
And God who clears the grounding berg and steers the grinding floe,
He hears the cry of the little kit-fox and the lemming on the snow.
But since our women must walk gay and money buys their gear,
The sealing-boats they filch that way at hazard year by year.
English they be and Japanee that hang on the Brown Bear's flank,
And some be Scot, but the worst, God wot, and the boldest thieves, be Yank!

It was the sealer Northern Light, to the Smoky Seas she bore.
With a stovepipe stuck from a starboard port and the Russian flag at her fore.
(Baltic, Stralsund, and Northern Light—oh! they were birds of a feather—
Slipping away to the Smoky Seas, three seal-thieves together!)
And at last she came to a sandy cove and the Baltic lay therein,
But her men were up with the herding seal to drive and club and skin.
There were fifteen hundred skins abeach, cool pelt and proper fur,
When the Northern Light drove into the bight and the sea-mist drove with her.
The Baltic called her men and weighed—she could not choose but run—
For a stovepipe seen through the closing mist, it shows like a four-inch gun
(And loss it is that is sad as death to lose both trip and ship
And lie for a rotting contraband on Vladivostock slip).
She turned and dived in the sea-smother as a rabbit dives in the whins,
And the Northern Light sent up her boats to steal the stolen skins.
They had not brought a load to side or slid their hatches clear,
When they were aware of a sloop-of-war, ghost-white and very near.
Her flag she showed, and her guns she showed—three of them, black, abeam,
And a funnel white with the crusted salt, but never a show of steam.
There was no time to man the brakes, they knocked the shackle free,
And the Northern Light stood out again, goose-winged to open sea.

(For life it is that is worse than death, by force of Russian law
To work in the mines of mercury that loose the teeth in your jaw!)
They had not run a mile from shore—they heard no shots behind—
When the skipper smote his hand on his thigh and threw her up in the wind:
"Bluffed—raised out on a bluff," said he, "for if my name's Tom Hall,
You must set a thief to catch a thief—and a thief has caught us all!
By every butt in Oregon and every spar in Maine,
The hand that spilled the wind from her sail was the hand of Reuben Paine!
He has rigged and trigged her with paint and spar, and, faith, he has faked her well—
But I'd know the Stralsund's deckhouse yet from here to the booms o' Hell.
Oh, once we ha' met at Baltimore, and twice on Boston pier,

But the sickest day for you, Reuben Paine, was the day that you came here—
The day that you came here, my lad, to scare us from our seal
With your funnel made o' your painted cloth, and your guns o' rotten deal!
Ring and blow for the Baltic now, and head her back to the bay,
For we'll come into the game again with a double deck to play!"

They rang and blew the sealers' call—the poaching cry o' the sea—
And they raised the Baltic out of the mist, and an angry ship was she:
And blind they groped through the whirling white, and blind to the bay again,
Till they heard the creak of the Stralsund's boom and the clank of her mooring-chain.
They laid them down by bitt and boat, their pistols in their belts,
And: "Will you fight for it, Reuben Paine, or will you share the pelts?"

A dog-toothed laugh laughed Reuben Paine, and bared his flenching knife.
"Yea, skin for skin, and all that he hath a man will give for his life;
But I've six thousand skins below, and Yeddo Port to see,
And there's never a law of God or man runs north of Fifty-Three.
So go in peace to the naked seas with empty holds to fill,
And I'll be good to your seal this catch, as many as I shall kill."

Answered the snap of a closing lock and the jar of a gun-butt slid,
But the tender fog shut fold on fold to hide the wrong they did.
The weeping fog rolled fold on fold the wrath of man to cloak,
And the flame-spurts pale ran down the rail as the sealing-rifles spoke.
The bullets bit on bend and butt, the splinter slivered free,
(Little they trust to sparrow-dust that stop the seal in his sea!)
The thick smoke hung and would not shift, leaden it lay and blue,
But three were down on the Baltic's deck and two of the Stralsund's crew.
An arm's length out and overside the banked fog held them bound;
But, as they heard or groan or word, they fired at the sound.
For one cried out on the name of God, and one to have him cease;
And the questing volley found them both and bade them hold their peace.
And one called out on a heathen joss and one on the Virgin's Name;
And the schooling bullet leaped across and showed them whence they came.
And in the waiting silences the rudder whined beneath,
And each man drew his watchful breath slow taken 'tween the teeth—
Trigger and ear and eye acock, knit brow and hard-drawn lips—
Bracing his feet by chock and cleat for the rolling of the ships:
Till they heard the cough of a wounded man that fought in the fog for breath,
Till they heard the torment of Reuben Paine that wailed upon his death:

"The tides they'll go through Fundy Race but I'll go never more
And see the hogs from ebb-tide mark turn scampering back to shore.
No more I'll see the trawlers drift below the Bass Rock ground,
Or watch the tall Fall steamer lights tear blazing up the Sound.
Sorrow is me, in a lonely sea and a sinful fight I fall,
But if there's law o' God or man you'll swing for it yet, Tom Hall!"

Tom Hall stood up by the quarter-rail. "Your words in your teeth," said he.
"There's never a law of God or man runs north of Fifty Three.
So go in grace with Him to face, and an ill-spent life behind,
And I'll take care o' your widows, Rube, as many as I shall find."
A Stralsund man shot blind and large, and a warlock Finn was he,
And he hit Tom Hall with a bursting ball a hand's-breadth over the knee.
Tom Hall caught hold by the topping-lift, and sat him down with an oath,
"You'll wait a little, Rube," he said, "the Devil has called for both.
The Devil is driving both this tide, and the killing-grounds are close,
And we'll go up to the Wrath of God as the holluschickie goes.
O men, put back your guns again and lay your rifles by,
We've fought our fight, and the best are down. Let up and let us die!
Quit firing, by the bow there—quit! Call off the Baltic's crew!
You're sure of Hell as me or Rube—but wait till we get through."

There went no word between the ships, but thick and quick and loud
The life-blood drummed on the dripping decks, with the fog-dew from the shroud,
The sea-pull drew them side by side, gunnel to gunnel laid,
And they felt the sheerstrakes pound and clear, but never a word was said.

Then Reuben Paine cried out again before his spirit passed:
"Have I followed the sea for thirty years to die in the dark at last?
Curse on her work that has nipped me here with a shifty trick unkind—
I have gotten my death where I got my bread, but I dare not face it blind.
Curse on the fog! Is there never a wind of all the winds I knew
To clear the smother from off my chest, and let me look at the blue?"
The good fog heard—like a splitten sail, to left and right she tore,
And they saw the sun-dogs in the haze and the seal upon the shore.
Silver and gray ran spit and bay to meet the steel-backed tide,
And pinched and white in the clearing light the crews stared overside.
O rainbow-gay the red pools lay that swilled and spilled and spread,
And gold, raw gold, the spent shell rolled between the careless dead—
The dead that rocked so drunkenwise to weather and to lee,
And they saw the work their hands had done as God had bade them see!

And a little breeze blew over the rail that made the headsails lift,
But no man stood by wheel or sheet, and they let the schooners drift.
And the rattle rose in Reuben's throat and he cast his soul with a cry,
And "Gone already?" Tom Hall he said. "Then it's time for me to die."
His eyes were heavy with great sleep and yearning for the land,
And he spoke as a man that talks in dreams, his wound beneath his hand.
"Oh, there comes no good in the westering wind that backs against the sun;
Wash down the decks—they're all too red—and share the skins and run,
Baltic, Stralsund, and Northern Light,—clean share and share for all,
You'll find the fleets off Tolstoi Mees, but you will not find Tom Hall.
Evil he did in shoal-water and blacker sin on the deep,
But now he's sick of watch and trick, and now he'll turn and sleep.
He'll have no more of the crawling sea that made him suffer so,

But he'll lie down on the killing-grounds where the holluschickie go.
And west you'll turn and south again, beyond the sea-fog's rim,
And tell the Yoshiwara girls to burn a stick for him.
And you'll not weight him by the heels and dump him overside,
But carry him up to the sand-hollows to die as Bering died,
And make a place for Reuben Paine that knows the fight was fair,
And leave the two that did the wrong to talk it over there!"

Half-steam ahead by guess and lead, for the sun is mostly veiled—
Through fog to fog, by luck and log, sail ye as Bering sailed;
And, if the light shall lift aright to give your landfall plain,
North and by west, from Zapne Crest, ye raise the Crosses Twain.
Fair marks are they to the inner bay, the reckless poacher knows,
What time the scarred see-catchie lead their sleek seraglios.
Ever they hear the floe-pack clear, and the blast of the old bull-whale,
And the deep seal-roar that beats off shore above the loudest gale.
Ever they wait the winter's hate as the thundering boorga calls,
Where northward look they to St. George, and westward to St. Paul's.
Ever they greet the hunted fleet—lone keels off headlands drear—
When the sealing-schooners flit that way at hazard year by year.
Ever in Yokohama Port men tell the tale anew
Of a hidden sea and a hidden fight,
When the Baltic ran from the Northern Light
And the Stralsund fought the two!

THE DERELICT

"And reports the derelict Mary Pollock still at sea."
Shipping News.

I was the staunchest of our fleet
Till the Sea rose beneath our feet
Unheralded, in hatred past all measure.
Into his pits he stamped my crew,
Buffeted, blinded, bound and threw;
Bidding me eyeless wait upon his pleasure.

Man made me, and my will
Is to my maker still,
Whom now the currents con, the rollers steer—
Lifting forlorn to spy
Trailed smoke along the sky,
Falling afraid lest any keel come near.

Wrenched as the lips of thirst,
Wried, dried, and split and burst,

Bone-bleached my decks, wind-scoured to the graining;
And, jarred at every roll,
The gear that was my soul
Answers the anguish of my beams' complaining.

For life that crammed me full,
Gangs of the prying gull
That shriek and scrabble on the riven hatches.
For roar that dumbed the gale
My hawse-pipes guttering wail,
Sobbing my heart out through the uncounted watches.

Blind in the hot blue ring
Through all my points I swing—
Swing and return to shift the sun anew.
Blind in my well-known sky
I hear the stars go by,
Mocking the prow that can not hold one true!

White on my wasted path
Wave after wave in wrath
Frets 'gainst his fellow, warring where to send me.
Flung forward, heaved aside,
Witless and dazed I bide
The mercy of the comber that shall end me.

North where the bergs careen,
The spray of seas unseen
Smokes round my head and freezes in the falling;
South where the corals breed,
The footless, floating weed
Folds me and fouls me, strake on strake upcrawling.

I that was clean to run
My race against the sun—
Strength on the deep, am bawd to all disaster—
Whipped forth by night to meet
My sister's careless feet,
And with a kiss betray her to my master!

Man made me, and my will
Is to my maker still—
To him and his, our peoples at their pier:
Lifting in hope to spy
Trailed smoke along the sky;
Falling afraid lest any keel come near!

You couldn't pack a Broadwood half a mile—
You mustn't leave a fiddle in the damp—
You couldn't raft an organ up the Nile,
And play it in an Equatorial swamp.
I travel with the cooking-pots and pails—
I'm sandwiched 'tween the coffee and the pork—
And when the dusty column checks and tails,
You should hear me spur the rearguard to a walk!

With my "Pilly-willy-winky-winky popp!"
[O it's any tune that comes into my head!]
So I keep 'em moving forward till they drop;
So I play 'em up to water and to bed.

In the silence of the camp before the fight,
When it's good to make your will and say your prayer,
You can hear my strumpty-tumpty overnight
Explaining ten to one was always fair.
I'm the prophet of the Utterly Absurd,
Of the Patently Impossible and Vain—
And when the Thing that Couldn't has occurred,
Give me time to change my leg and go again.

With my "Tumpa-tumpa-tumpa-tum-pa tump!"
In the desert where the dung-fed camp-smoke curled
There was never voice before us till I led our lonely chorus,
I—the war-drum of the White Man round the world!

By the bitter road the Younger Son must tread,
Ere he win to hearth and saddle of his own,—
'Mid the riot of the shearers at the shed,
In the silence of the herder's hut alone—
In the twilight, on a bucket upside down,
Hear me babble what the weakest won't confess—
I am Memory and Torment—I am Town!
I am all that ever went with evening dress!

With my "Tunk-a tunka-tunka-tunka-tunk!"
[So the lights—the London lights—grow near and plain!]
So I rowel 'em afresh towards the Devil and the Flesh,
Till I bring my broken rankers home again.

In desire of many marvels over sea,
Where the new-raised tropic city sweats and roars,
I have sailed with Young Ulysses from the quay

Till the anchor rumbled down on stranger shores.
He is blooded to the open and the sky,
He is taken in a snare that shall not fail,
He shall hear me singing strongly, till he die,
Like the shouting of a backstay in a gale.

With my "Hya! Heeya! Heeya! Hullah! Haul!"
[O the green that thunders aft along the deck!]
Are you sick o' towns and men? You must sign and sail again,
For it's "Johnny Bowlegs, pack your kit and trek!"

Through the gorge that gives the stars at noon-day clear—
Up the pass that packs the scud beneath our wheel—
Round the bluff that sinks her thousand fathom sheer—
Down the valley with our guttering brakes asqueal:
Where the trestle groans and quivers in the snow,
Where the many-shedded levels loop and twine,
So I lead my reckless children from below
Till we sing the Song of Roland to the pine.

With my "Tinka-tinka-tinka-tinka-tink!"
[And the axe has cleared the mountain, croup and crest!]
So we ride the iron stallions down to drink,
Through the cañons to the waters of the West!

And the tunes that mean so much to you alone—
Common tunes that make you choke and blow your nose,
Vulgar tunes that bring the laugh that brings the groan—
I can rip your very heartstrings out with those;
With the feasting, and the folly, and the fun—
And the lying, and the lusting, and the drink,
And the merry play that drops you, when you're done,
To the thoughts that burn like irons if you think.

With my "Plunka-lunka-lunka-lunka-lunk!"
Here's a trifle on account of pleasure past,
Ere the wit that made you win gives you eyes to see your sin
And the heavier repentance at the last.

Let the organ moan her sorrow to the roof—
I have told the naked stars the grief of man.
Let the trumpets snare the foeman to the proof—
I have known Defeat, and mocked it as we ran.
My bray ye may not alter nor mistake
When I stand to jeer the fatted Soul of Things,
But the Song of Lost Endeavour that I make,
Is it hidden in the twanging of the strings?

With my "Ta-ra-rara-rara-ra-ra-rrrp!"
[Is it naught to you that hear and pass me by?]
But the word—the word is mine, when the order moves the line
And the lean, locked ranks go roaring down to die.

The grandam of my grandam was the Lyre—
[O the blue below the little fisher-huts!]
That the Stealer stooping beach ward filled with fire,
Till she bore my iron head and ringing guts!
By the wisdom of the centuries I speak—
To the tune of yestermorn I set the truth—
I, the joy of life unquestioned—I, the Greek—
I, the everlasting Wonder Song of Youth!

With my "Tinka-tinka-tinka-tinka-tink!"
[What d'ye lack, my noble masters? What d'ye lack?]
So I draw the world together link by link:
Yea, from Delos up to Limerick and back!

"THE LINER SHE'S A LADY"

The Liner she's a lady, an' she never looks nor 'eeds—
The Man-o'-War's 'er 'usband, an' 'e gives 'er all she needs;
But, oh, the little cargo-boats, that sail the wet seas roun',
They're just the same as you an' me a-plyin' up an' down!

Plyin' up an' down, Jenny, 'angin' round the Yard,
All the way by Fratton tram down to Portsmouth 'Ard;
Anythin' for business, an' we're growin' old—
Plyin' up an' down, Jenny, waitin' in the cold!

The Liner she's a lady by the paint upon 'er face,
An' if she meets an accident they call it sore disgrace:
The Man-o'-War's 'er 'usband, and 'e's always 'andy by,
But, oh, the little cargo-boats! they've got to load or die.

The Liner she's a lady, and 'er route is cut an' dried;
The Man-o'-War's 'er 'usband, an' 'e always keeps beside;
But, oh, the little cargo-boats that 'aven't any man!
They've got to do their business first, and make the most they can.

The Liner she's a lady, and if a war should come,
The Man-o'-War's 'er 'usband, and 'e'd bid 'er stay at home;
But, oh, the little cargo-boats that fill with every tide!
'E'd 'ave to up an' fight for them, for they are England's pride.

The Liner she's a lady, but if she wasn't made,
There still would be the cargo-boats for 'ome an' foreign trade.
The Man-o'-War's 'er 'usband, but if we wasn't 'ere,
'E wouldn't have to fight at all for 'ome an' friends so dear.

'Ome an' friends so dear, Jenny, 'angin' round the Yard,
All the way by Fratton tram down to Portsmouth 'Ard;
Anythin' for business, an' we're growin' old—
'Ome an' friends so dear, Jenny, waitin' in the cold!

MULHOLLAND'S CONTRACT

The fear was on the cattle, for the gale was on the sea,
An' the pens broke up on the lower deck an' let the creatures free—
An' the lights went out on the lower deck, an' no one down but me.

I had been singin' to them to keep 'em quiet there,
For the lower deck is the dangerousest, requirin' constant care,
An' give to me as the strongest man, though used to drink and swear.

I see my chance was certain of bein' horned or trod,
For the lower deck was packed with steers thicker 'n peas in a pod,
An' more pens broke at every roll—so I made a Contract with God.

An' by the terms of the Contract, as I have read the same,
If He got me to port alive I would exalt His name,
An' praise His Holy Majesty till further orders came.

He saved me from the cattle an' He saved me from the sea,
For they found me 'tween two drownded ones where the roll had landed me—
An' a four-inch crack on top of my head, as crazy as could be.

But that were done by a stanchion, an' not by a bullock at all,
An' I lay still for seven weeks convalessing of the fall,
An' readin' the shiny Scripture texts in the Seamen's Hospital.

An' I spoke to God of our Contract, an' He says to my prayer:
"I never puts on My ministers no more than they can bear.
So back you go to the cattle-boats an' preach My Gospel there.

"For human life is chancy at any kind of trade,
But most of all, as well you know, when the steers are mad-afraid;
So you go back to the cattle-boats an' preach 'em as I've said.

"They must quit drinkin' an' swearin', they mustn't knife on a blow,
They must quit gamblin' their wages, and you must preach it so;

For now those boats are more like Hell than anything else I know."

I didn't want to do it, for I knew what I should get,
An' I wanted to preach Religion, handsome an' out of the wet,
But the Word of the Lord were lain on me, an' I done what I was set.

I have been smit an' bruisèd, as warned would be the case,
An' turned my cheek to the smiter exactly as Scripture says;
But following that, I knocked him down an' led him up to Grace.

An' we have preaching on Sundays whenever the sea is calm,
An' I use no knife nor pistol an' I never take no harm,
For the Lord abideth back of me to guide my fighting arm.

An' I sign for four pound ten a month and save the money clear,
An' I am in charge of the lower deck, an' I never lose a steer;
An' I believe in Almighty God an' I preach His Gospel here.

The skippers say I'm crazy, but I can prove 'em wrong,
For I am in charge of the lower deck with all that doth belong—
Which they would not give to a lunatic, and the competition so strong!

ANCHOR SONG

From Many Inventions

Heh! Walk her round. Heave, ah heave her short again!
Over, snatch her over, there, and hold her on the pawl.
Loose all sail, and brace your yards aback and full—
Ready jib to pay her off and heave short all!

Well, ah fare you well; we can stay no more with you, my love—
Down, set down your liquor and your girl from off your knee;
For the wind has come to say:
"You must take me while you may,
If you'd go to Mother Carey,
(Walk her down to Mother Carey!)
Oh, we're bound to Mother Carey where she feeds her chicks at sea!"

Heh! Walk her round. Break, ah break it out o' that!
Break our starboard bower out, apeak, awash, and clear.
Port—port she casts, with the harbour-roil beneath her foot,
And that's the last o' bottom we shall see this year!

Well, ah fare you well, for we've got to take her out again—
Take her out in ballast, riding light and cargo-free.

And it's time to clear and quit
When the hawser grips the bitt,
So we'll pay you with the foresheet and a promise from the sea!

Heh! Tally on! Aft and walk away with her!
Handsome to the cathead, now; O tally on the fall!
Stop, seize and fish, and easy on the davit-guy.
Up, well up the fluke of her, and inboard haul!

Well, ah fare you well, for the Channel wind's took hold of us,
Choking down our voices as we snatch the gaskets free.
And it's blowing up for night,
And she's dropping Light on Light,
And she's snorting under bonnets for a breath of open sea.

Wheel, full and by; but she'll smell her road alone to-night.
Sick she is and harbour-sick—O sick to clear the land!
Roll down to Brest with the old Red Ensign over us—
Carry on and thrash her out with all she'll stand!

Well, ah fare you well, and it's Ushant gives the door to us,
Whirling like a windmill on the dirty scud to lee:
Till the last, last flicker goes
From the tumbling water-rows,
And we're off to Mother Carey
(Walk her down to Mother Carey!)
Oh, we're bound for Mother Carey where she feeds her chicks at sea!

THE SEA-WIFE

There dwells a wife by the Northern Gate,
And a wealthy wife is she;
She breeds a breed o' rovin' men
And casts them over sea,

And some are drowned in deep water,
And some in sight o' shore.
And word goes back to the weary wife,
And ever she sends more.

For since that wife had gate and gear,
And hearth and garth and bield,
She willed her sons to the white harvest,
And that is a bitter yield.

She wills her sons to the wet ploughing,

To ride the horse of tree;
And syne her sons come home again
Far-spent from out the sea.

The good wife's sons come home again
With little into their hands,
But the lore of men that ha' dealt with men
In the new and naked lands.

But the faith of men that ha' brothered men
By more than the easy breath,
And the eyes o' men that ha' read wi' men
In the open books of death.

Rich are they, rich in wonders seen,
But poor in the goods o' men,
So what they ha' got by the skin o' their teeth
They sell for their teeth again.

For whether they lose to the naked skin,
Or win to their hearts' desire,
They tell it all to the weary wife
That nods beside the fire.

Her hearth is wide to every wind
That makes the white ash spin;
And tide and tide and 'tween the tides
Her sons go out and in;

(Out with great mirth that do desire
Hazard of trackless ways,
In with content to wait their watch
And warm before the blaze);

And some return by failing light,
And some in waking dream,
For she hears the heels of the dripping ghosts
That ride the rough roof-beam.

Home, they come home from all the ports,
The living and the dead;
The good wife's sons come home again
For her blessing on their head!

HYMN BEFORE ACTION

The earth is full of anger,
The seas are dark with wrath;
The Nations in their harness
Go up against our path!
Ere yet we loose the legions—
Ere yet we draw the blade,
Jehovah of the Thunders,
Lord God of Battles, aid!

High lust and froward bearing,
Proud heart, rebellious brow—
Deaf ear and soul uncaring,
We seek Thy mercy now:
The sinner that forswore Thee,
The fool that passed Thee by,
Our times are known before Thee—
Lord, grant us strength to die!

For those who kneel beside us
At altars not Thine own,
Who lack the lights that guide us,
Lord, let their faith atone;
If wrong we did to call them,
By honour bound they came;
Let not Thy wrath befall them,
But deal to us the blame.

From panic, pride, and terror,
Revenge that knows no rein—
Light haste and lawless error,
Protect us yet again.
Cloak Thou our undeserving,
Make firm the shuddering breath,
In silence and unswerving
To taste thy lesser death!

Ah, Mary pierced with sorrow,
Remember, reach and save
The soul that comes to-morrow
Before the God that gave!
Since each was born of woman,
For each at utter need—
True comrade and true foeman,
Madonna, intercede!

E'en now their vanguard gathers,
E'en now we face the fray—
As Thou didst help our fathers,

Help Thou our host to-day!
Fulfilled of signs and wonders,
In life, in death made clear—
Jehovah of the Thunders,
Lord God of Battles, hear!

TO THE TRUE ROMANCE

From Many Inventions

Thy face is far from this our war,
Our call and counter-cry,
I shall not find Thee quick and kind,
Nor know Thee till I die:
Enough for me in dreams to see
And touch Thy garments' hem:
Thy feet have trod so near to God
I may not follow them.

Through wantonness if men profess
They weary of Thy parts,
E'en let them die at blasphemy
And perish with their arts;
But we that love, but we that prove
Thine excellence august,
While we adore discover more
Thee perfect, wise, and just.

Since spoken word Man's Spirit stirred
Beyond his belly-need,
What is is Thine of fair design
In thought and craft and deed;
Each stroke aright of toil and fight,
That was and that shall be,
And hope too high, wherefore we die,
Has birth and worth in Thee.

Who holds by Thee hath Heaven in fee
To gild his dross thereby,
And knowledge sure that he endure
A child until he die—
For to make plain that man's disdain
Is but new Beauty's birth—
For to possess, in loneliness,
The joy of all the earth.

As Thou didst teach all lovers speech,
And Life all mystery,
So shalt Thou rule by every school
Till love and longing die,
Who wast or yet the lights were set,
A whisper in the Void,
Who shalt be sung through planets young
When this is clean destroyed.

Beyond the bounds our staring rounds,
Across the pressing dark,
The children wise of outer skies
Look hitherward and mark
A light that shifts, a glare that drifts,
Rekindling thus and thus,
Not all forlorn, for Thou hast borne
Strange tales to them of us.

Time hath no tide but must abide
The servant of Thy will;
Tide hath no time, for to Thy rhyme
The ranging stars stand still—
Regent of spheres that lock our fears
Our hopes invisible,
Oh 'twas certes at Thy decrees
We fashioned Heaven and Hell!

Pure Wisdom hath no certain path
That lacks thy morning-eyne,
And captains bold by Thee controlled
Most like to Gods design;
Thou art the Voice to kingly boys
To lift them through the fight,
And Comfortress of Unsuccess,
To give the dead good-night—

A veil to draw 'twixt God His Law
And Man's infirmity,
A shadow kind to dumb and blind
The shambles where we die;
A sum to trick th' arithmetic
Too base of leaguing odds,
The spur of trust, the curb of lust,
Thou handmaid of the Gods!

Oh Charity, all patiently
Abiding wrack and scaith!
Oh Faith, that meets ten thousand cheats

Yet drops no jot of faith!
Devil and brute Thou dost transmute
To higher, lordlier show,
Who art in sooth that lovely Truth
The careless angels know!

Thy face is far from this our war,
Our call and counter-cry,
I may not find Thee quick and kind,
Nor meet Thee till I die.

Yet may I look with heart unshook
On blow brought home or missed—
Yet may I hear with equal ear
The clarions down the list;
Yet set my lance above mischance
And ride the barriere—
Oh, hit or miss, how little 'tis,
My Lady is not there!

THE FLOWERS

"To our private taste, there is always something a little exotic, almost artificial, in songs which, under an English aspect and dress, are yet so manifestly the product of other skies. They affect us like translations; the very fauna and flora are alien, remote; the dog's-tooth violet is but an ill substitute for the rathe primrose, nor can we ever believe that the wood-robin sings as sweetly in April as the English thrush."— The Athenæum.

Buy my English posies—
Kent and Surrey may,
Violets of the Undercliff
Wet with Channel spray;
Cowslips from a Devon combe
Midland furze afire—
Buy my English posies,
And I'll sell your hearts' desire!

Buy my English posies!—
You that scorn the may
Won't you greet a friend from home
Half the world away?
Green against the draggled drift,
Faint and frail and first—
Buy my Northern blood-root
And I'll know where you were nursed!
Robin down the logging-road whistles, "Come to me,"

Spring has found the maple-grove, the sap is running free;
All the winds o' Canada call the ploughing-rain.
Take the flower and turn the hour, and kiss your love again!

Buy my English posies!—
Here's to match your need.
Buy a tuft of royal heath,
Buy a bunch of weed
White as sand of Muysenberg
Spun before the gale—
Buy my heath and lilies
And I'll tell you whence you hail!
Under hot Constantia broad the vineyards lie—
Throned and thorned the aching berg props the speckless sky—
Slow below the Wynberg firs trails the tilted wain—
Take the flower and turn the hour, and kiss your love again!

Buy my English posies!—
You that will not turn,
Buy my hot-wood clematis,
Buy a frond o' fern
Gathered where the Erskine leaps
Down the road to Lorne—
Buy my Christmas creeper
And I'll say where you were born!
West away from Melbourne dust holidays begin—
They that mock at Paradise woo at Cora Lynn—
Through the great South Otway gums sings the great South Main—
Take the flower and turn the hour, and kiss your love again!

Buy my English posies!—
Here's your choice unsold!
Buy a blood-red myrtle-bloom,
Buy the kowhai's gold
Flung for gift on Taupo's face
Sign that spring is come—
Buy my clinging myrtle
And I'll give you back your home!
Broom behind the windy town; pollen o' the pine—
Bell-bird in the leafy deep where the ratas twine—
Fern above the saddle-bow, flax upon the plain—
Take the flower and turn the hour, and kiss your love again!

Buy my English posies!
Ye that have your own
Buy them for a brother's sake
Overseas, alone.
Weed ye trample underfoot

Floods his heart abrim—
Bird ye never heeded,
Oh, she calls his dead to him!
Far and far our homes are set round the Seven Seas.
Woe for us if we forget, we that hold by these!
Unto each his mother-beach, bloom and bird and land—
Masters of the Seven Seas, oh, love and understand!

THE LAST RHYME OF TRUE THOMAS

The King has called for priest and cup,
The King has taken spur and blade
To dub True Thomas a belted knight,
And all for the sake o' the songs he made.

They have sought him high, they have sought him low,
They have sought him over down and lea;
They have found him by the milk-white thorn
That guards the gates o' Faerie.

'Twas bent beneath and blue above,
Their eyes were held that they might not see
The kine that grazed between the knowes,
Oh, they were the Queens o' Faerie!

"Now cease your song," the King he said,
"Oh, cease your song and get you dight
To vow your vow and watch your arms,
For I will dub you a belted knight.

"For I will give you a horse o' pride,
Wi' blazon and spur and page and squire;
Wi' keep and tail and seizin and law,
And land to hold at your desire."

True Thomas smiled above his harp,
And turned his face to the naked sky,
Where, blown before the wastrel wind,
The thistle-down she floated by.

"I ha' vowed my vow in another place,
And bitter oath it was on me,
I ha' watched my arms the lee-long night,
Where five-score fighting-men would flee.

"My lance is tipped o' the hammered flame,

My shield is beat o' the moonlight cold;
And I won my spurs in the Middle World,
A thousand fathoms beneath the mould.

"And what should I make wi' a horse o' pride,
And what should I make wi' a sword so brown,
But spill the rings o' the Gentle Folk
And flyte my kin in the Fairy Town?

"And what should I make wi' blazon and belt,
Wi' keep and tail and seizin and fee,
And what should I do wi' page and squire
That am a king in my own countrie?

"For I send east and I send west,
And I send far as my will may flee,
By dawn and dusk and the drinking rain,
And syne my Sendings return to me.

"They come wi' news of the groanin' earth,
They come wi' news o' the roarin' sea,
Wi' word of Spirit and Ghost and Flesh,
And man that's mazed among the three."

The King he bit his nether lip,
And smote his hand upon his knee:
"By the faith o' my soul, True Thomas," he said,
"Ye waste no wit in courtesie!

"As I desire, unto my pride,
Can I make Earls by three and three,
To run before and ride behind
And serve the sons o' my body."

"And what care I for your row-foot earls,
Or all the sons o' your body?
Before they win to the Pride o' Name,
I trow they all ask leave o' me.

"For I make Honour wi' muckle mouth,
As I make Shame wi' mincin' feet,
To sing wi' the priests at the market-cross,
Or run wi' the dogs in the naked street.

"And some they give me the good red gold,
And some they give me the white money,
And some they give me a clout o' meal,
For they be people o' low degree.

"And the song I sing for the counted gold
The same I sing for the white money,
But best I sing for the clout o' meal
That simple people given me."

The King cast down a silver groat,
A silver groat o' Scots money,
"If I come with a poor man's dole," he said,
"True Thomas, will ye harp to me?"

"Whenas I harp to the children small,
They press me close on either hand:
And who are you," True Thomas said,
"That you should ride while they must stand?

"Light down, light down from your horse o' pride,
I trow ye talk too loud and hie,
And I will make you a triple word,
And syne, if ye dare, ye shall 'noble me."

He has lighted down from his horse o' pride,
And set his back against the stone.
"Now guard you well," True Thomas said,
"Ere I rax your heart from your breast-bone!"

True Thomas played upon his harp,
The fairy harp that couldna' lee,
And the first least word the proud King heard,
It harpit the salt tear out o' his ee.

"Oh, I see the love that I lost long syne,
I touch the hope that I may not see,
And all that I did o' hidden shame,
Like little snakes they hiss at me.

"The sun is lost at noon—at noon!
The dread o' doom has grippit me.
True Thomas, hide me under your cloak,
God wot, I'm little fit to dee!"

'Twas bent beneath and blue above—
'Twas open field and running flood—
Where, hot on heath and dyke and wall,
The high sun warmed the adder's brood.

"Lie down, lie down," True Thomas said.
"The God shall judge when all is done;

But I will bring you a better word
And lift the cloud that I laid on."

True Thomas played upon his harp,
That birled and brattled to his hand,
And the next least word True Thomas made,
It garred the King take horse and brand.

"Oh, I hear the tread o' the fighting-men,
I see the sun on splent and spear!
I mark the arrow outen the fern!
That flies so low and sings so clear!

"Advance my standards to that war,
And bid my good knights prick and ride;
The gled shall watch as fierce a fight
As e'er was fought on the Border side!"

'Twas bent beneath and blue above,
'Twas nodding grass and naked sky,
Where ringing up the wastrel wind
The eyass stooped upon the pye.

True Thomas sighed above his harp,
And turned the song on the midmost string;
And the last least word True Thomas made
He harpit his dead youth back to the King.

"Now I am prince, and I do well
To love my love withouten fear;
To walk wi' man in fellowship,
And breathe my horse behind the deer.

"My hounds they bay unto the death,
The buck has couched beyond the burn,
My love she waits at her window
To wash my hands when I return.

"For that I live am I content
(Oh! I have seen my true love's eyes!)
To stand wi' Adam in Eden-glade,
And run in the woods o' Paradise!"

'Twas nodding grass and naked sky,
'Twas blue above and bent below,
Where, checked against the wastrel wind,
The red deer belled to call the doe.

True Thomas laid his harp away,
And louted low at the saddle-side;
He has taken stirrup and hauden rein,
And set the King on his horse o' pride.

"Sleep ye or wake," True Thomas said,
"That sit so still, that muse so long;
Sleep ye or wake?—till the latter sleep
I trow ye'll not forget my song.

"I ha' harpit a shadow out o' the sun
To stand before your face and cry;
I ha' armed the earth beneath your heel,
And over your head I ha' dusked the sky!

"I ha' harpit ye up to the Throne o' God,
I ha' harpit your secret soul in three;
I ha' harpit ye down to the Hinges o' Hell,
And—ye—would—make—a Knight o' me!"

THE STORY OF UNG

Once, on a glittering ice-field, ages and ages ago,
Ung, a maker of pictures, fashioned an image of snow.
Fashioned the form of a tribesman—gaily he whistled and sung,
Working the snow with his fingers. Read ye the Story of Ung!

Pleased was his tribe with that image—came in their hundreds to scan—
Handled it, smelt it, and grunted: "Verily, this is a man!
Thus do we carry our lances—thus is a war-belt slung.
Ay, it is even as we are. Glory and honour to Ung!"

Later he pictured an aurochs—later he pictured a bear—
Pictured the sabre-tooth tiger dragging a man to his lair—
Pictured the mountainous mammoth, hairy, abhorrent, alone—
Out of the love that he bore them, scribing them clearly on bone.

Swift came the tribe to behold them, peering and pushing and still—
Men of the berg-battered beaches, men of the boulder-hatched hill,
Hunters and fishers and trappers—presently whispering low;
"Yea, they are like—and it may be.... But how does the Picture-man know?

"Ung—hath he slept with the Aurochs—watched where the Mastodon roam?
Spoke on the ice with the Bow-head—followed the Sabre-tooth home?
Nay! These are toys of his fancy! If he have cheated us so,
How is there truth in his image—the man that he fashioned of snow?"

Wroth was that maker of pictures—hotly he answered the call:
"Hunters and fishers and trappers, children and fools are ye all!
Look at the beasts when ye hunt them!" Swift from the tumult he broke,
Ran to the cave of his father and told him the shame that they spoke.

And the father of Ung gave answer, that was old and wise in the craft,
Maker of pictures aforetime, he leaned on his lance and laughed:
"If they could see as thou seest they would do what thou hast done,
And each man would make him a picture, and—what would become of my son?

"There would be no pelts of the reindeer, flung down at thy cave for a gift,
Nor dole of the oily timber that strands with the Baltic drift;
No store of well-drilled needles, nor ouches of amber pale;
No new-cut tongues of the bison, nor meat of the stranded whale.

"Thou hast not toiled at the fishing when the sodden trammels freeze,
Nor worked the war-boats outward, through the rush of the rock-staked seas,
Yet they bring thee fish and plunder—full meal and an easy bed—
And all for the sake of thy pictures." And Ung held down his head.

"Thou hast not stood to the aurochs when the red snow reeks of the fight;
Men have no time at the houghing to count his curls aright:
And the heart of the hairy mammoth thou sayest they do not see,
Yet they save it whole from the beaches and broil the best for thee.

"And now do they press to thy pictures, with open mouth and eye,
And a little gift in the doorway, and the praise no gift can buy:
But—sure they have doubted thy pictures, and that is a grievous stain—
Son that can see so clearly, return them their gifts again."

And Ung looked down at his deerskins—their broad shell-tasselled bands—
And Ung drew downward his mitten and looked at his naked hands;
And he gloved himself and departed, and he heard his father, behind:
"Son that can see so clearly, rejoice that thy tribe is blind!"

Straight on that glittering ice-field, by the caves of the lost Dordogne,
Ung, a maker of pictures, fell to his scribing on bone—
Even to mammoth editions. Gaily he whistled and sung,
Blessing his tribe for their blindness. Heed ye the Story of Ung!

THE THREE-DECKER

"The three-volume novel is extinct"

Full thirty foot she towered from waterline to rail.
It cost a watch to steer her, and a week to shorten sail;
But, spite all modern notions, I found her first and best—
The only certain packet for the Islands of the Blest.

Fair held our breeze behind us—'twas warm with lovers' prayers:
We'd stolen wills for ballast and a crew of missing heirs;
They shipped as Able Bastards till the Wicked Nurse confessed,
And they worked the old three-decker to the Islands of the Blest.

Carambas and serapés we waved to every wind,
We smoked good Corpo Bacco when our sweethearts proved unkind;
With maids of matchless beauty and parentage unguessed
We also took our manners to the Islands of the Blest.

We asked no social questions—we pumped no hidden shame—
We never talked obstetrics when the little stranger came:
We left the Lord in Heaven, we left the fiends in Hell.
We weren't exactly Yussufs, but—Zuleika didn't tell!

No moral doubt assailed us, so when the port we neared,
The villain got his flogging at the gangway, and we cheered.
'Twas fiddles in the foc'sle—'twas garlands on the mast,
For every one got married, and I went ashore at last.

I left 'em all in couples akissing on the decks.
I left the lovers loving and the parents signing checks.
In endless English comfort by county-folk caressed,
I left the old three-decker at the Islands of the Blest!

That route is barred to steamers: you'll never lift again
Our purple-painted headlands or the lordly keeps of Spain.
They're just beyond the skyline, howe'er so far you cruise
In a ram-you-damn-you liner with a brace of bucking screws.

Swing round your aching search-light—'twill show no haven's peace!
Ay, blow your shrieking sirens to the deaf, gray-bearded seas!
Boom out the dripping oil-bags to skin the deep's unrest—
But you aren't a knot the nearer to the Islands of the Blest.

And when you're threshing, crippled, with broken bridge and rail,
On a drogue of dead convictions to hold you head to gale,
Calm as the Flying Dutchman, from truck to taffrail dressed,
You'll see the old three-decker for the Islands of the Blest.

You'll see her tiering canvas in sheeted silver spread;
You'll hear the long-drawn thunder 'neath her leaping figure-head;
While far, so far above you, her tall poop-lanterns shine

Unvexed by wind or weather like the candles round a shrine.

Hull down—hull down and under—she dwindles to a speck,
With noise of pleasant music and dancing on her deck.
All's well—all's well aboard her—she's dropped you far behind,
With a scent of old-world roses through the fog that ties you blind.

Her crew are babes or madmen? Her port is all to make?
You're manned by Truth and Science, and you steam for steaming's sake?
Well, tinker up your engines—you know your business best—
She's taking tired people to the Islands of the Blest!

AN AMERICAN

The American Spirit speaks:

If the Led Striker call it a strike,
Or the papers call it a war,
They know not much what I am like,
Nor what he is, my Avatar.

Through many roads, by me possessed,
He shambles forth in cosmic guise;
He is the Jester and the Jest,
And he the Text himself applies.

The Celt is in his heart and hand,
The Gaul is in his brain and nerve;
Where, cosmopolitanly planned,
He guards the Redskin's dry reserve.

His easy unswept hearth he lends
From Labrador to Guadeloupe;
Till, elbowed out by sloven friends,
He camps, at sufferance, on the stoop.

Calm-eyed he scoffs at sword and crown,
Or panic-blinded stabs and slays:
Blatant he bids the world bow down,
Or cringing begs a crumb of praise;

Or, sombre-drunk, at mine and mart,
He dubs his dreary brethren Kings.
His hands are black with blood: his heart
Leaps, as a babe's, at little things.

But, through the shift of mood and mood,
Mine ancient humour saves him whole—
The cynic devil in his blood
That bids him mock his hurrying soul;

That bids him flout the Law he makes,
That bids him make the Law he flouts,
Till, dazed by many doubts, he wakes
The drumming guns that—have no doubts;

That checks him foolish hot and fond,
That chuckles through his deepest ire,
That gilds the slough of his despond
But dims the goal of his desire;

Inopportune, shrill-accented,
The acrid Asiatic mirth
That leaves him careless 'mid his dead,
The scandal of the elder earth.

How shall he clear himself, how reach
Our bar or weighed defence prefer—
A brother hedged with alien speech
And lacking all interpreter?

Which knowledge vexes him a space;
But while reproof around him rings,
He turns a keen untroubled face
Home, to the instant need of things.

Enslaved, illogical, elate,
He greets th' embarrassed Gods, nor fears
To shake the iron hand of Fate
Or match with Destiny for beers.

Lo! imperturbable he rules,
Unkempt, disreputable, vast—
And, in the teeth of all the schools
I—I shall save him at the last!

THE MARY GLOSTER

I've paid for your sickest fancies; I've humoured your crackedest whim—
Dick, it's your daddy—dying: you've got to listen to him!
Good for a fortnight, am I? The doctor told you? He lied.
I shall go under by morning, and—Put that nurse outside.

Never seen death yet, Dickie? Well, now is your time to learn,
And you'll wish you held my record before it comes to your turn.
Not counting the Line and the Foundry, the yards and the village, too,
I've made myself and a million; but I'm damned if I made you.
Master at two-and-twenty, and married at twenty three—
Ten thousand men on the pay-roll, and forty freighters at sea!
Fifty years between 'em, and every year of it fight,
And now I'm Sir Anthony Gloster, dying, a baronite:
For I lunched with His Royal 'Ighness—what was it the papers a-had?
"Not least of our merchant-princes." Dickie, that's me, your dad!
I didn't begin with askings. I took my job and I stuck;
And I took the chances they wouldn't, an' now they're calling it luck.
Lord, what boats I've handled—rotten and leaky and old!
Ran 'em, or—opened the bilge-cock, precisely as I was told.
Grub that 'ud bind you crazy, and crews that 'ud turn you gray,
And a big fat lump of insurance to cover the risk on the way.
The others they duresn't do it; they said they valued their life
(They've served me since as skippers). I went, and I took my wife.
Over the world I drove 'em, married at twenty-three,
And your mother saving the money and making a man of me.
I was content to be master, but she said there was better behind;
She took the chances I wouldn't, and I followed your mother blind.
She egged me to borrow the money, an' she helped me clear the loan,
When we bought half shares in a cheap 'un and hoisted a flag of our own.
Patching and coaling on credit, and living the Lord knew how,
We started the Red Ox freighters—we've eight-and-thirty now.
And those were the days of clippers, and the freights were clipper-freights,
And we knew we were making our fortune, but she died in Macassar Straits—
By the Little Paternosters, as you come to the Union Bank—
And we dropped her in fourteen fathom; I pricked it off where she sank.
Owners we were, full owners, and the boat was christened for her,
And she died out there in childbed. My heart, how young we were!
So I went on a spree round Java and well-nigh ran her ashore,
But your mother came and warned me and I wouldn't liquor no more.
Strict I stuck to my business, afraid to stop or I'd think,
Saving the money (she warned me), and letting the other men drink.
And I met McCullough in London (I'd saved five 'undred then),
And 'tween us we started the Foundry—three forges and twenty men:
Cheap repairs for the cheap 'uns. It paid, and the business grew,
For I bought me a steam-lathe patent, and that was a gold mine too.
"Cheaper to build 'em than buy 'em," I said, but McCullough he shied,
And we wasted a year in talking before we moved to the Clyde.
And the Lines were all beginning, and we all of us started fair,
Building our engines like houses and staying the boilers square.
But McCullough 'e wanted cabins with marble and maple and all,
And Brussels and Utrecht velvet, and baths and a Social Hall,
And pipes for closets all over, and cutting the frames too light.
But McCullough he died in the Sixties, and—Well, I'm dying to-night....

I knew—I knew what was coming, when we bid on the Byfleet's keel.
They piddled and piffled with iron: I'd given my orders for steel.
Steel and the first expansions. It paid, I tell you, it paid,
When we came with our nine-knot freighters and collared the long-run trade.
And they asked me how I did it, and I gave 'em the Scripture text,
"You keep your light so shining a little in front o' the next!"
They copied all they could follow, but they couldn't copy my mind,
And I left 'em sweating and stealing a year and a half behind.
Then came the armour-contracts, but that was McCullough's side;
He was always best in the Foundry, but better, perhaps, he died.
I went through his private papers; the notes was plainer than print;
And I'm no fool to finish if a man'll give me a hint.
(I remember his widow was angry.) So I saw what the drawings meant,
And I started the six-inch rollers, and it paid me sixty per cent.
Sixty per cent with failures, and more than twice we could do,
And a quarter-million to credit, and I saved it all for you.
I thought—it doesn't matter—you seemed to favour your ma,
But you're nearer forty than thirty, and I know the kind you are.
Harrer an' Trinity College! I ought to ha' sent you to sea—
But I stood you an education, an' what have you done for me?
The things I knew was proper you wouldn't thank me to give,
And the things I knew was rotten you said was the way to live;
For you muddled with books and pictures, an' china an' etchin's an' fans,
And your rooms at college was beastly—more like a whore's than a man's—
Till you married that thin-flanked woman, as white and as stale as a bone,
And she gave you your social nonsense; but where's that kid o' your own?
I've seen your carriages blocking the half of the Cromwell Road,
But never the doctor's brougham to help the missus unload.
(So there isn't even a grandchild, an' the Gloster family's done.)
Not like your mother, she isn't. She carried her freight each run.
But they died, the pore little beggars! At sea she had 'em—they died.
Only you, an' you stood it; you haven't stood much beside—
Weak, a liar, and idle, and mean as a collier's whelp
Nosing for scraps in the galley. No help—my son was no help!
So he gets three 'undred thousand, in trust and the interest paid.
I wouldn't give it you, Dickie—you see, I made it in trade.
You're saved from soiling your fingers, and if you have no child,
It all comes back to the business. Gad, won't your wife be wild!
Calls and calls in her carriage, her 'andkerchief up to 'er eye:
"Daddy! dear daddy's dyin'!" and doing her best to cry.
Grateful? Oh, yes, I'm grateful, but keep 'er away from here.
Your mother 'ud never ha' stood 'er, and, anyhow, women are queer....
There's women will say I've married a second time. Not quite!
But give pore Aggie a hundred, and tell her your lawyers'll fight.
She was the best o' the boiling—you'll meet her before it ends;
I'm in for a row with the mother—I'll leave you settle my friends:
For a man he must go with a woman, which women don't understand—
Or the sort that say they can see it they aren't the marrying brand.

But I wanted to speak o' your mother that's Lady Gloster still.
I'm going to up and see her, without it's hurting the will.
Here! Take your hand off the bell-pull. Five thousand's waiting for you,
If you'll only listen a minute, and do as I bid you do.
They'll try to prove me a loony, and, if you bungle, they can;
And I've only you to trust to! (O God, why ain't he a man?)
There's some waste money on marbles, the same as McCullough tried—
Marbles and mausoleums—but I call that sinful pride.
There's some ship bodies for burial—we've carried 'em, soldered and packed;
Down in their wills they wrote it, and nobody called them cracked.
But me—I've too much money, and people might.... All my fault:
It come o' hoping for grandsons and buying that Wokin' vault.
I'm sick o' the 'ole dam' business; I'm going back where I came.
Dick, you're the son o' my body, and you'll take charge o' the same!
I'm going to lie by your mother, ten thousand mile away,
And they'll want to send me to Woking; and that's where you'll earn your pay.
I've thought it out on the quiet, the same as it ought to be done—
Quiet, and decent, and proper—an' here's your orders, my son.
You know the Line? You don't, though. You write to the Board, and tell
Your father's death has upset you an' you're goin' to cruise for a spell,
An' you'd like the Mary Gloster—I've held her ready for this—
They'll put her in working order an' you'll take her out as she is.
Yes, it was money idle when I patched her and put her aside
(Thank God, I can pay for my fancies!)—the boat where your mother died,
By the Little Paternosters, as you come to the Union Bank,
We dropped her—I think I told you—and I pricked it off where she sank.
[Tiny she looked on the grating—that oily, treacly sea—]
Hundred and eighteen East, remember, and South just three.
Easy bearings to carry—three South—three to the dot;
But I gave McAndrews a copy in case of dying—or not.
And so you'll write to McAndrews, he's Chief of the Maori Line;
They'll give him leave, if you ask 'em and say it's business o' mine.
I built three boats for the Maoris, an' very well pleased they were,
An' I've known Mac since the Fifties, and Mac knew me—and her.
After the first stroke warned me I sent him the money to keep
Against the time you'd claim it, committin' your dad to the deep;
For you are the son o' my body, and Mac was my oldest friend,
I've never asked 'im to dinner, but he'll see it out to the end.
Stiff-necked Glasgow beggar, I've heard he's prayed for my soul,
But he couldn't lie if you paid him, and he'd starve before he stole.
He'll take the Mary in ballast—you'll find her a lively ship;
And you'll take Sir Anthony Gloster, that goes on his wedding-trip,
Lashed in our old deck-cabin with all three port-holes wide,
The kick o' the screw beneath him and the round blue seas outside!
Sir Anthony Gloster's carriage—our 'ouse-flag flyin' free—
Ten thousand men on the pay-roll and forty freighters at sea!
He made himself and a million, but this world is a fleetin' show,
And he'll go to the wife of 'is bosom the same as he ought to go.

By the heel of the Paternosters—there isn't a chance to mistake—
And Mac'll pay you the money as soon as the bubbles break!
Five thousand for six weeks' cruising, the stanchest freighter afloat,
And Mac he'll give you your bonus the minute I'm out o' the boat!
He'll take you round to Macassar, and you'll come back alone;
He knows what I want o' the Mary.... I'll do what I please with my own.
Your mother 'ud call it wasteful, but I've seven-and-thirty more;
I'll come in my private carriage and bid it wait at the door....
For my son 'e was never a credit: 'e muddled with books and art,
And 'e lived on Sir Anthony's money and 'e broke Sir Anthony's heart.
There isn't even a grandchild, and the Gloster family's done—
The only one you left me, O mother, the only one!
Harrer an' Trinity College! Me slavin' early an' late,
An' he thinks I'm dyin' crazy, and you're in Macassar Strait!
Flesh o' my flesh, my dearie, for ever an' ever amen,
That first stroke come for a warning; I ought to ha' gone to you then,
But—cheap repairs for a cheap 'un—the doctors said I'd do:
Mary, why didn't you warn me? I've allus heeded to you,
Excep'—I know—about women; but you are a spirit now;
An', wife, they was only women, and I was a man. That's how.
An' a man 'e must go with a woman, as you could not understand;
But I never talked 'em secrets. I paid 'em out o' hand.
Thank Gawd, I can pay for my fancies! Now what's five thousand to me,
For a berth off the Paternosters in the haven where I would be?
I believe in the Resurrection, if I read my Bible plain,
But I wouldn't trust 'em at Wokin'; we're safer at sea again.
For the heart it shall go with the treasure—go down to the sea in ships.
I'm sick of the hired women—I'll kiss my girl on her lips!
I'll be content with my fountain, I'll drink from my own well,
And the wife of my youth shall charm me—an' the rest can go to Hell!
(Dickie, he will, that's certain.) I'll lie in our standin'-bed,
An' Mac'll take her in ballast—and she trims best by the head....
Down by the head an' sinkin'. Her fires are drawn and cold,
And the water's splashin' hollow on the skin of the empty hold—
Churning an' choking and chuckling, quiet and scummy and dark—
Full to her lower hatches and risin' steady. Hark!
That was the after-bulkhead ... she's flooded from stem to stern....
Never seen death yet, Dickie?... Well, now is your time to learn!

SESTINA OF THE TRAMP-ROYAL

Speakin' in general, I 'ave tried 'em all,
The 'appy roads that take you o'er the world.
Speakin' in general, I 'ave found them good
For such as cannot use one bed too long,
But must get 'ence, the same as I 'ave done,

An' go observin' matters till they die.

What do it matter where or 'ow we die,
So long as we've our 'ealth to watch it all—
The different ways that different things are done,
An' men an' women lovin' in this world—
Takin' our chances as they come along,
An' when they ain't, pretendin' they are good?

In cash or credit—no, it ain't no good;
You 'ave to 'ave the 'abit or you'd die,
Unless you lived your life but one day long,
Nor didn't prophesy nor fret at all,
But drew your tucker some'ow from the world,
An' never bothered what you might ha' done.

But, Gawd, what things are they I 'aven't done?
I've turned my 'and to most, an' turned it good,
In various situations round the world—
For 'im that doth not work must surely die;
But that's no reason man should labour all
'Is life on one same shift; life's none so long.

Therfore, from job to job I've moved along.
Pay couldn't 'old me when my time was done,
For something in my 'ead upset me all,
Till I 'ad dropped whatever 'twas for good,
An', out at sea, be'eld the dock-lights die,
An' met my mate—the wind that tramps the world.

It's like a book, I think, this bloomin' world,
Which you can read and care for just so long,
But presently you feel that you will die
Unless you get the page you're readin' done,
An' turn another—likely not so good;
But what you're after is to turn 'em all.

Gawd bless this world! Whatever she 'ath done—
Excep' when awful long—I've found it good.
So write, before I die, "'E liked it all!"

Rudyard Kipling – A Short Biography

Born in Bombay on 30th December 1865, Joseph Rudyard Kipling wrote short stories, poems and novels, a body of work whose reputation is in constant flux as his presentations and interpretations of empire are viewed within the changing context of empirical absolution in the twentieth century. Having spent the first five years of his life in India he felt a natural affinity for the country, though his upbringing had a distinctly colonial taste flavour. He was born in the Bombay Presidency of British India to Lockwood Kipling, an English art teacher and illustrator who took a position as professor of architectural sculpture in the Jeejeebhoy School of Art and Alice MacDonald, spoken of by the a Viceroy of India that "dullness and Mrs Kipling cannot exist in the same room". Though their presence in India was principally artistic and educational, rather than political, the company they kept and the establishments in which they kept it indicate an existence very much benefitting from the British Empire. Lockwood would later go on to assume a position as curator of the Lahore Museum, while working on various illustrations for Rudyard's writing, and various decorations for the Victoria and Albert museum in London. Much of his work, then, was coloured by the empire, whether in service to or benefitting from, and it was into this distinctly British experience of India that Rudyard was born.

Lockwood and Alice had met and fallen in love at Rudyard Lake in Rudyard, Staffordshire, and their affections for the area were so great they chose to refer to the lake in naming their first-born. Alice came from a family of four sisters, all of whose marriages were significant and well-arranged; moreover, Rudyard's most famous relative was Stanley Baldwin, Conservative Prime Minister on three occasions in the 1920s and 1930s. Kipling's sense of belonging in Bombay is found in 'To the City of Bombay' in the dedication to Seven Seas, a collection of poems published in 1900, which reads:—

> Mother of Cities to me,
> For I was born in her gate,
> Between the palms and the sea,
> Where the world-end steamers wait.

His parents considered themselves Anglo-Indians, and he would later assume this classification although he did not live there long. His first five years, which he describes as days of "strong light and darkness", ended when he and his three-year-old sister Alice were removed to Southsea, Plymouth, to board with Captain Pryse Agar Holloway and his wife Mrs Sarah Holloway, a couple who cared for the children of couples born in British India. They were there for six years and Kipling would later recall their time there with horror, describing incidents of cruelty and neglect and wondering whether it was these which speeded up his literary maturity, for "it made me give attention to the lies I soon found it necessary to tell: and this, I presume, is the foundation of literary effort".

Alice's time, by contrast, was relatively comfortable, Mrs Holloway hoping that she would marry her son, though this ambition would not come to fruition. They did have relatives in England, a maternal aunt Georgiana and her husband who lived in Fulham, London, in a house at which they spent a month each Christmas and which Kipling later described as "a paradise which I verily believe saved me". Their mother returned in 1877 and removed them from their custody with the Holloways. A year later he gained admission to the United Services College at Westward Ho! in Devon, a recently established school with the intention of readying boys for military service in the British Army. His time here was fraught physically, though emotionally it proved fruitful for he began several firm friendships with other boys at the school. Moreover, he found in it inspiration for the setting of his series of schoolboy stories, Stalky and Co, begun in 1899. Meanwhile, his sister Alice had returned to Southsea and was boarding with Florence Garrard, with whom he fell in love and on whom he modeled Maisie in his first novel, The Light That Failed, published in 1891. At sixteen he was found lacking in the academic perspicacity necessary to undertake a scholarship to Oxford University, his parents meanwhile lacking the wherewithal to finance him therein. As such his father sought a job for him in Lahore, Punjab, where he was now a museum curator. The position he found for his son was as assistant editor of the Civil and

Military Gazette, a small local newspaper. Kipling left for India on 20th September 1882, arriving in Bombay on 18th October. "There were yet three or four days" rail to Lahore, where my people lived. After these, my English years fell away, nor ever, I think, came back in full strength".

The Gazette appeared six days of the week, year-round save for a short break at both Christmas and Easter. Its editor Stephen Wheeler was diligent but Kipling's writing was insatiable, and he came to consider the paper his "mistress and most true love". In the summer of 1883 Kipling visited Shimla, the colonial hill-station and summer capital of British India which was then called Simla. Chosen by the British owing to its resemblance of English climate and scenery (as far as was possible in India), it became the seat of the Viceroy of India for the six months on the plains which were too hot for the British temperament, and subsequently became a "centre of power as well as pleasure". Lockwood was asked to serve in the Church there, and his family became yearly visitors while Kipling himself would take his annual leave here from 1885-88. The value of this time is evident from the regularity with which Simla appears in his writing for the Gazette, which in his journals he describes the time as

> "….pure joy—every golden hour counted. It began in heat and discomfort, by rail and road. It ended in the cool evening, with a wood fire in one's bedroom, and next morn—thirty more of them ahead!—the early cup of tea, the Mother who brought it in, and the long talks of us all together again."

In 1886, his Departmental Ditties appeared, his first collection of verse, and brought with it a change of editor; Kay Robinson, Wheeler's replacement, was in favour of Kipling's creativity and granted him more freedom in that respect, even asking him to write short stories to appear in the newspaper. The vivacity of his writing was captured in a description of him by an ex-colleague at the Gazette, saying he "never knew such a fellow for ink—he simply revelled in it, filling up his pen viciously, and then throwing the contents all over the office, so that it was almost dangerous to approach him". While in Lahore, he had thirty-nine stories published in the Gazette between November 1886 and June 1887. Most of these are compiled in Plain Tales from the Hills, his first collection of prose, which was published in January 1888 in Calcutta, shortly after his 22nd birthday. In November 1887, he transferred from the Gazette to its much larger sister newspaper, The Pioneer, based in Allahabad. The pace of his writing remained, and in 1888 he published six collections of stories, Soldiers Three, The Story of the Gadsbys, In Black and White, Under the Deodars, The Phantom Rickshaw and Wee Willie Winkie, composed of some 41 stories. In addition, his position as The Pioneer's special correspondent in the Western region of Rajputna, he wrote many sketches which were later compiled in Letters of Marque and published in From Sea to Sea and Other Sketches, Letters of Travel.

A dispute in 1889 saw him discharged from The Pioneer, though by now he had been considering his future and sold the rights to his six volumes of stories for £200 and a small royalty, while the Plain Tales fetched £50, along with six months' salary from The Pioneer in lieu of notice. Using the money to undertake a pilgrimage to London, the literary centre of the British Empire, he left India on 9th March 1889, travelling via Rangoon, San Francisco, Hong Kong and Japan, then through the United States writing articles for The Pioneer which were also included in From Sea to Sea and Other Sketches, Letters of Travel. Arriving in England at Liverpool on October 1889, London and his literary début there beckoned.

His first task was to find a place to live, and he eventually settled on quarters in Villiers Street, Strand. The next two years saw several stories accepted by various magazine editors, the publication of the novel The Light That Failed, a nervous breakdown, the collaboration with Wolcott Balestier on the novel (uncharacterstically misspelt) The Naulhaka, and in 1891, following his doctors' advice, he embarked on a further sea voyage, travelling to South Africa, Australia, New Zealand and also returning to India. His plans to spend Christmas with his family were cut short on the news of Balestier's sudden death from typhoid fever, prompting an immediate return to London. Before he left, he had proposed to Balestier's sister Caroline Starr Balestier, with whom he had been having a hushed romance for just over a year. Back in London, Life's Handicap was published in 1891, a collection of short stories whose subject was the British in India, and British India. On 18th January 1892 aged 26 he married Caroline in the midst of an epidemic of influenza. Caroline was given away by Henry James, the famous and celebrated American author.

Honeymooning in Japan, they travelled via Vermont, America, to visit the Balestier estate, and upon arrival in Yokahama they found that their bank, The New Oriental Banking Corporation, had failed, though this loss did not deter them and they returned to Vermont, Caroline now pregnant with their first child. Renting a cottage on a farm for $10 per month, they lived a spartan existence and were "extraordinarily and self-centredly content". The named the residence Bliss Cottage, and it was here that the child was born, named Josephine, "in three foot of snow on the night of 29th December 1892. Her Mother's birthday being the 31st and mine the 30th we congratulated her on her sense of the fitness of things." While here, Kipling had his first ideas for the Jungle Books. Shortly after Josephine was born the couple moved in pursuit of more space and comfort, buying ten acres overlooking the Connecticut River from Caroline's brother. The house they built there was inspired by the Mughul architecture he encountered in Lahore, and was named Naulakha (this time correctly spelt) in honour of Wolcott. His literary output in four years here included the Jungle Books, a collection of short stories entitled The Day's Work, the novel Captain Courageous and a plethora of poetry, of which most notably the volume The Seven Seas and his Barrack-Room Ballads. Meanwhile, he enjoyed correspondence with the many children who wrote to him about the Jungle Books.

In between this writing, Kipling took regular visitors. Most notably Arthur Conan Doyle came, bringing golf clubs and staying for two days to give Kipling an extended golf lesson. Kipling enjoyed the game so much that he continued to play, even in winter with special red balls, though he found that the ice would lead to drives travelling two miles as they slid "down the long slope to the Connecticut River". Elsie, the couple's second daughter, was born in February 1896, and by this time it is thought that their marriage had lost its original spark of spontaneity and descended into routine, though they remained loyal to one another. By now, failed arbitration between the United States and England over a border dispute involving British Guiana incited Anglo-American tensions which, in May 1896, resulted in a confrontation between Kipling and Caroline's brother, resulting in his arrest and, in the hearing which followed, the destruction of Kipling's private life, leaving him exhausted and miserable and leading to their return to England.

They had settled Torquay, Devon, by September 1896, and he remained socially present and literarily productive. The success of his writing had brought him fame, and he had responded with a sense of duty to include in his writing elements of political persuasion, most notably in his two poems Recessional and The White Man's Burden, which caused controversy when they were published in 1897 and 1899 respectively. Many considered them anthemic to the empire, propaganda for the imperial mindset so prevalent in the Victoria era. Their first son, John, was born in August 1887. Another journey to South Africa began a tradition of wintering there, which continued until 1908. His reputation as Poet of the Empire saw him well-received by politicians in the Cape Colony, and he started the newspaper The Friend for Lord Roberts and the British troops in Bloemfontein. Back in England, they moved to Rottingdean, East Sussex, in 1897, and in 1902 he bought Bateman's, a house built in 1630, which was his home from until his death in 1936. Kim was published in 1902, after which he collected material for Just So Stories for Little Children, published a year later. Both he and Josephine developed pneumonia while visiting the United States, from which she later died.

This decade proved his most successful, being awarded the Nobel Prize for Literature in 1907, the prize citation reading "in consideration of the power of observation, originality of imagination, virility of ideas and remarkable talent for narration which characterise the creations of this world-famous author". He was the first English-language recipient. At the award ceremony in Switzerland, Carl David af Wirsén praised Kipling and the English literary tradition:

> The Swedish Academy, in awarding the Nobel Prize in Literature this year to Rudyard Kipling, desires to pay a tribute to the literature of England, so rich in manifold glories, and to the greatest genius in the realm of narrative that that country has produced in our times.

Following this achievement, Kipling published Rewards and Fairies, which contained If, voted Britain's favourite poem in a BBC opinion poll in 1995. He turned down several recommendations for knighthood and was considered for Poet Laureate, though this position was never offered to him.

The sense of perseverance, honour and stoicism in If prevailed in many of his opinions, including that on the First World War. Writing in The New Army in Training in 1915, he scorned those who refused conscription, considering

> ....what will be the position in years to come of the young man who has deliberately elected to outcaste himself from this all-embracing brotherhood? What of his family, and, above all, what of his descendants, when the books have been closed and the last balance struck of sacrifice and sorrow in every hamlet, village, parish, suburb, city, shire, district, province, and Dominion throughout the Empire?

This attitude saw him encourage his son, John, to go to war, and he was promptly killed at the Battle of Loos in September 1915, aged 18. Last seen during the battle stumbling blindly through the mud, screaming in agony after an exploding shell had ripped his face apart, Kipling would write—

"If any question why we died
Tell them, because our fathers lied"

—perhaps betraying the guilt he felt at encouraging his son to go to war and finding him a position in the Irish Guards through his friendship with commander-in-chief Lord Roberts, for whom he had established The Friend in Bloemfontein. His death inspired much of Kipling's successive writing, notably My Boy Jack and a two-volume history of the Irish Guards, considered one of the finest examples of regimental history. Ironically, though his writing and his political position had arguably cost John his life, after the war he became friends with a French soldier whose copy of Kim, kept in his breast pocket, had stopped a bullet and saved his life. For a while the book and the soldier's Croix de Guerre were with Kipling, presented as tokens of gratitude, and they remained in contact, though when Kipling learned of the soldier's child he insisted on returning both book and medal.

He kept writing until 1930, though at a considerably slower pace, and to less success. His death, already once incorrectly announced early by a magazine in a premature obituary (and to which he responded

"I've just read that I am dead. Don't forget to delete me from your list of subscribers") came on 18th January 1936, at the age of 70, from a perforated duodenal ulcer. His coffin was carried by, among others, his cousin the Prime Minister Stanley Baldwin, and his marble casket covered by a Union flag. He was cremated at Golders Green Crematorium in Northwest London and his ashes are buried at Poets' Corner in Westminster Abbey, alongside the graves of both Charles Dickens and Thomas Hardy.

In conjunction with various earthly memorials which commemorate him, alongside his extensive writing, he has a crater on Mercury named after him. The question of memorial and monument is much-addressed in English Literature and, as various great authors and poets have agreed before Kipling's time, his memory lives on more vivaciously set in his words, far longer and better represented than it could set in stone.

Rudyard Kipling - A Concise Bibliography

Books
The City of Dreadful Night (1885, short story)
Plain Tales from the Hills (1888)
Soldiers Three (1888)
The Story of the Gadsbys (1888)
In Black and White (1888)
Under the Deodars (1888)
The Phantom 'Rickshaw and other Eerie Tales (1888)
Wee Willie Winkie and Other Child Stories (1888)
Life's Handicap (1891)
The Light that Failed (1891) (novel)
American Notes (1891) (non-fiction)
The Naulahka: A Story of West and East (1892) (with Wolcott Balestie)
Many Inventions (1893)
The Jungle Book (1894)
Mowgli's Brothers (short story)
Kaa's Hunting (short story)
Tiger! Tiger! (short story)
The White Seal (short story)
Rikki-Tikki-Tavi (short story)
Toomai of the Elephants (short story)
Her Majesty's Servants (originally titled Servants of the Queen) (short story)
The Second Jungle Book (1895)
How Fear Came (short story)
The Miracle of Purun Bhagat (short story)
Letting in the Jungle (short story)
The Undertakers (short story)
The King's Ankus (short story)
Quiquern (short story)
Red Dog" (short story)
The Spring Running (short story)
Captains Courageous (1896) (novel)

The Day's Work (1898)
A Fleet in Being (1898)
Stalky & Co. (1899)
From Sea to Sea and Other Sketches, Letters of Travel (1899) (non-fiction)
Kim (1901) (novel)
Just So Stories for Little Children (1902)
Traffics and Discoveries (1904) (24 collected short stories)
With the Night Mail (1905) A Story of 2000 A.D
Puck of Pook's Hill (1906)
The Brushwood Boy (1907)
Actions and Reactions (1909)
A Song of the English (1909) (with W. Heath Robinson illustrator)
Rewards and Fairies (1910)
A History of England (1911) (non-fiction with Charles Robert Leslie Fletcher)
Songs from Books (1912)
As Easy as A.B.C. (1912) (Science-fiction short story)
The Fringes of the Fleet (1915) (non-fiction)
Sea Warfare (1916) (non-fiction)
A Diversity of Creatures (1917)
Land and Sea Tales for Scouts and Guides (1923)
The Irish Guards in the Great War (1923) (non-fiction)
Debits and Credits (1926)
A Book of Words (1928) (non-fiction)
Thy Servant a Dog (1930)
Limits and Renewals (1932)
Tales of India: the Windermere Series (1935)
Something of Myself (1937) (autobiography)
The Elephant's Child (fiction)

Autobiographies and Speeches
A Book of Words (1928)
Something of Myself (1937)

Short Story Collections
Quartette (1885) – with his father, mother, and sister
Plain Tales from the Hills (1888)
Soldiers Three, The Story of the Gadsbys, In Black and White (1888)
The Phantom 'Rickshaw and other Eerie Tales (1888)
Under the Deodars (1888)
Wee Willie Winkie and Other Child Stories (1888)
Life's Handicap (1891)
Many Inventions (1893)
The Jungle Book (1894)
The Second Jungle Book (1895)
The Day's Work (1898)
Life's Handicap (1899)

Stalky & Co. (1899)
Just So Stories (1902)
Traffics and Discoveries (1904)
Puck of Pook's Hill (1906)
Actions and Reactions (1909)
Abaft the Funnel (1909)
Rewards and Fairies (1910)
The Eyes of Asia (1917)
A Diversity of Creatures (1917)
Land and Sea Tales for Scouts and Guides (1923)
Debits and Credits (1926)
Thy Servant a Dog (1930)
Limits and Renewals (1932)

Military Collections
A Fleet in Being (1898)
France at War (1915)
The New Army in Training (1915)
Sea Warfare (1916)
The War in the Mountains (1917)
The Graves of the Fallen (1919)
The Irish Guards in the Great War (1923)

Poetry Collections
Schoolboy Lyrics (1881)
Echoes (1884) – with his sister, Alice ('Trix')
Departmental Ditties (1886)
Barrack-Room Ballads (1890)
The Seven Seas (1896)
An Almanac of Twelve Sports (1898, with illustrations by William Nicholson)
The Five Nations (1903)
Collected Verse (1907)
Songs from Books (1912)
The Years Between (1919)
Rudyard Kipling's Verse: Definitive Edition (1940)
The Muse Among the Motors (poetry)

Travel Writing
From Sea to Sea – Letters of Travel: 1887–1889 (1899)
Letters of Travel: 1892–1913 (1920)
Souvenirs of France (1933)
Brazilian Sketches: 1927 (1940)

Collected Works

The Outward Bound Edition (1897–1937, 36 volumes)
The Edition de Luxe (1897–1937, 38 volumes)
The Bombay Edition (1913–38, 31 volumes)
The Sussex Edition (1937–39, 35 volumes)
The Burwash Edition (1941, 28 volumes)

Poems

Departmental Ditties and Other Verses (1886)
Barrack Room Ballads (1889, republished with additions at later times)
The Seven Seas and Further Barrack-Room Ballads (In various editions 1891–96)
The Five Nations (with some new and some reprinted and revised poems, 1903)
Twenty-two original 'Historical Poems' (1911)
Songs from Books (1912)
The Years Between (1919)

Posthumous Collections

Rudyard Kipling's Verse: Definitive edition
A Choice of Kipling's Verse, edited by T.S. Eliot

In addition Kipling wrote and published many hundreds of poems too numerous to include here.

www.ingramcontent.com/pod-product-compliance
Lightning Source LLC
Chambersburg PA
CBHW032031040426
42448CB00027B/1194